Praise for *Midlife Is Not a Crisis*

Midlife Is Not a Crisis—it is a chrysalis—and the proverbial butterfly that emerges from its pages is depth-full, magical, and rare. This delight-full book shows you how and why to age and live juicily and inspires you to fully live your radiant life at every stage. This marvelous book is a poetic and educational journey about juicy aging, and how to prepare, prosper, and thrive in the second half of life, and it also beautifully applies to all the stages of living and growing.

—SARK co-author and artist of *Succulent Wild Love*
and creator of *PlanetSARK.com*

"In *Midlife Is Not a Crisis*, astrologer Virginia Bell has written a consequential, compelling book that roadmaps life as an unfolding journey and reveals the purpose and heart of each life phase as an opportunity for creative change. Based on the cycles of the planets, this is a practical yet lyrical guide to the stages of life through the language of astrology and the power of its timing and the wisdom of new paradigms beautifully carved from myth, archetype, and real life.

"*Midlife Is Not a Crisis* will inspire you to find renewal of purpose and amazing, unique opportunities for self-discovery at every age and the rich, ripe fruit of wisdom that lovingly connects you with the elder within awaiting at each cycle, honoring each as the doorway to a higher soul consciousness. Virginia Bell has written a classic, a book that will empower you to thrive in all the stages of your life."

—Ronnie Grishman, editor-in-chief, *Dell Horoscope Magazine*

D1264652

"What a clear, practical, and totally fascinating guide for how to thrive in all the phases of your life! With her brilliant mastery of astrology, Virginia Bell gives you the map to navigate your entire life and to become your fully authentic self. Keep this book on your bedside table!"

—Jean Haner, author of *Your Hidden Symmetry:*
How Your Birth Date Reveals the Plan for Your Life and
The Wisdom of Your Face: Change Your Life with Chinese Face Reading

"Appealing to master astrologers and avid horoscope readers, Virginia Bell looks brilliantly at the heavens and sees in the stars a spiritual road map revealing where we come from, where we are now, what lies ahead if we pay attention to the signs, and what's likely to happen if we don't. Midlife is not a crisis and neither is any turning point in life once we, too, open this book and take an enlightening look at the heavens above in order to understand soulfully what's happening below."

—Karol Jackowski, author of bestseller
Ten Fun Things to Do Before You Die

"The world is awash in information right now, but starving for wisdom. Virginia Bell's book on the astrology of maturity is utterly timely. It is a thorough, well-written guide to the loving cultivation of the wise elder within each of us."

—Jessica Murray, author of *Soul-Sick Nation: An Astrologer's View of*
America and *At the Crossroads: An Astrologer Looks*
at These Turbulent Times, and creator of *MotherSky.com*

"With her ageless wisdom, Virginia Bell has written a book for the ages. Using astrology's key cycles, she shows us that life has a plot and that its unfolding will give you new-found opportunities for growth. No matter what stage of life you are in, however, her book, *Midlife Is Not a Crisis,* is for the young-at-heart, for it will inspire you to embrace the changes and challenges you face with courage and a sense of adventure."

—Shirley Soffer, author of *The Astrology Sourcebook: Your Guide to*
Understanding the Symbolic Language of the Stars

"Sigmund Freud may have introduced us to the 'mid-life crisis,' but he left us high and dry when he led us to believe that it's all downhill from there. In a culture that has been deliberately 'youth-anized' by the media, it's time to open our eyes to what astrologers have always known: that time, repetition, and experience are the only teachers here. From our perspective, the so-called mid-life crisis is, in fact, the entrance to higher levels of wisdom and experience. With that said, I am here to applaud Virginia Bell. With *Midlife Is Not a Crisis*, she has tapped into the 'Secret of the Ages': little did we know that life really does begin at forty. It may come as even more of a surprise that no one has enough experience or wisdom to become consciously aware of their life's purpose, until they turn fifty. If we live to be sixty, a whole other realm of consciousness opens up. From that point on, the heart and the soul and the mind enter realms that are inaccessible to those who have not lived long enough to go there. YES! There is life after the mid-life crisis. It is where the sidewalk ends and real life begins. This is a worthwhile book that will be a boon to astrologers, psychologists, and laymen alike. Now that the world is over-populated with Baby-Boomers, Ms. Bell will find a receptive audience for a book that could be just what the doctor ordered for anyone who suffers from the belief that 'You can't trust anyone over thirty' and life is over and done with on the day we turn forty."

—Cal Garrison, author of *The Astrology of 2012 and Beyond*
and *The Old Girls' Book of Spells: The Real Meaning of Menopause, Sex, Car Keys, and Other Important Stuff About Magic*

"A generation or two ago, people expected to work at their jobs until age 59 or 65, if they were lucky, receive a gold watch, and *possibly* look forward to a few more years subsisting on Social Security or whatever they managed to save. But things have changed. Many of us live well into our 80s and even 90s and are enjoying marvelous second and third acts AND new careers. Virginia Bell's *Midlife Is Not a Crisis: Using Astrology to Thrive in the Second Half of Life* has arrived right on time to serve and inspire Boomers, Gen-Xers, and anyone planning to make the most of the awakening that occurs at 40–45 and give it their all after age 50.

"The book begins with a fabulous primer for astrology newbies (deliciously well-written and an enjoyable review of the basics for veterans) and then forays into the much needed and under-discussed planetary transits and patterns that all 60-, 70- and 80-somethings experience. Virginia leaves no stone unturned as she provides a precise and uplifting road map with which to navigate and enrich one's golden years."

—Shelley L. Ackerman, astrologer, author,
actor, entertainer at *www.karmicrelief.com*

"It's easy to be depressed about getting old, rather than optimistic. That's why I love Virginia Bell's book *Midlife Is Not a Crisis: Using Astrology to Thrive in the Second Half of Life* because it lets readers know—whether they are 29 or 84—that it's never too late for happiness. Virginia shows us what to expect during common life cycles and how to navigate their challenges for desired self-transformation."

—Judika Illes, author of *Encyclopedia of 5000 Spells, The Big Book of Practical Spells, and the Encyclopedia of Mystics, Saints, and Sages*

MIDLIFE
IS NOT A
CRISIS

using astrology to thrive in the second half of life

VIRGINIA BELL

foreword by Steven Forrest

WEISER BOOKS

This edition first published in 2017 by Weiser Books, an imprint of
Red Wheel/Weiser, LLC
With offices at:
65 Parker Street, Suite 7
Newburyport, MA 01950
www.redwheelweiser.com

ISBN: 978-1-57863-612-9
Library of Congress Cataloging-in-Publication Data available upon
request.

Cover design by Kathryn Sky-Peck
Interior by Frame25 Productions
Typeset in Garamond Premier Pro

Printed in the United States of America
M&G
10 9 8 7 6 5 4 3 2 1

CONTENTS

Foreword by Steven Forrest   ix

Acknowledgments   xiii

Introduction   xv

Introduction to the Cycles: Our Power Years   1

An Overview of Astrology: The Birth Chart   5

THE CYCLES

The Saturn Return: Growing Up and Getting Real (Age 29)   39

The Midlife Journey: Breakdowns
and Breakthroughs (Ages 37–45)   73

The Chiron Return: The Youth of Old Age (Ages 49–51)   105

The Second Saturn Return: The New Elder (Age 58)   129

The Closing Uranus Square: A Second Wind (Ages 62–63)   157

The Seventies: Real Problems, Real Possibilities   183

The Uranus Return at Eighty-Four: The Homecoming   209

Appendix: Profiles   227

Suggested Reading   237

FOREWORD

In the interest of journalistic transparency, I do need to report that Virginia Bell is much older than me—well, five and a half years older anyway. I therefore bow before her venerable wisdom when it comes to life's passages; and—giggles aside—a compassionate, wise look at life's passages through the clear lens of astrology is the subject of this very fine volume.

To further preserve my integrity, before I launch into the heart of this foreword, I should add that I am biased. I have loved Virginia Bell since the moment I met her. That was at an astrological conference in Connecticut, probably a quarter century ago. I had mailed her several recorded readings before that, so I "knew" her in that strange way an astrologer gets to know someone via hieroglyphics on a sheet of paper. But when we met face to face, the karmic violins played. Miracle of miracles, in that moment, the main meeting hall at the conference hotel cleared of every soul.

That simple fact demonstrates one basic truth about Virginia Bell—as befits her Sun/Moon conjunction in the magical eighth house, Ginnie wields some serious *ju-ju*. The crowd went poof. She and I were left standing there solo, without interruption, talking and connecting, and I was impressed on a whole other level. I also felt as if we had known each other for a thousand years. Which is probably the approximate truth of the matter.

All this of course makes it sound like Virginia Bell and I were "an item," but it wasn't like that. There was never a grand romance or even a "moment" for that matter. Instead of skidding down that slippery Romeo and Juliet slope, we instead planted our four Earth-sign feet upon the solid ground of that human masterpiece: a lifelong friendship—one that has now stood for nearly half my life.

In the fashion of friendship, there has always been a sense of spiritual parity between Ginnie and me. I would turn to her for help or perspective as easily as she would turn to me. Over the years, I have confidently referred many clients to her. When she decided to become a student in my apprenticeship program, I had a moment of feeling as if the Dalai Lama had asked me for meditation tips. I was flattered and a little disoriented. Ginnie is a true wise woman. Read any page at random in this excellent book, and you will immediately see what I mean. What could I possibly teach her? But one of Virginia Bell's virtues is her ability to learn something from everyone she meets—and again, these pages will demonstrate that to you.

Albert Einstein famously said, "When you are courting a nice girl, an hour seems like a second. When you sit on a redhot cinder, a second seems like an hour. That's relativity." Well, our clearing that room at the conference in Connecticut seems like it just happened yesterday. We were both in mid-life then—and now we are gray-haired and wrinkled enough that younger folks fancy us wise. Life goes by so quickly. Those words have become a cliché. Pronounce them in front of a group of intelligent young people in their twenties, and they all sagaciously nod their heads. And they *do* understand—but not as they will understand when they are fifty or seventy.

There are plenty of fine young astrologers today—and no shortage of pontificating old fools. Age itself teaches us very little. But one point is sure: those fine young astrologers will mostly be even better with another few decades of experience. That is true in general but especially so when it comes to the actual subject of this book: life's chronological milestones. It really helps to have experienced them personally before we speak about them! Only an arrogant young fool, destined to become an annoying old one, would argue against that idea.

I vividly recall the vague sense of illegitimacy I had at age thirty while talking to a wise "old" man or woman about the meaning of the Second Saturn Return at about one's fifty-ninth birthday. I laugh to remember that one of my struggles back then was to avoid speaking of their lives in the past tense. Such are the illusions of youth . . .

Robbie Robertson put it so well in one of his solo tunes: "We grow up so slowly, and we grow old so fast." I guess everyone over fifty would agree with that line. What makes the difference though are the usual pivotal questions: Have we honestly examined our own experiences? Have we taken responsibility for the repeating patterns in our lives? Have we actually gotten anything deeper than mere memory from them? Did we acknowledge our own errors truthfully enough to have learned from them? Did we love, and dare, and occasionally fly though fog on pure faith with no plan B and no parachute?

No one can answer those questions about another soul. But I am going to ditch my parachute and take off in the fog anyway. Virginia Bell has lived that way. She embodies these human virtues with humility, grace, and—blessedly—with a naughty twinkle in her eye.

Many a tree has been turned to pulp in order to rehash old astrological ideas and print them yet again under a new title. This is not one of those books. In these pages, a wise woman has left us a treasure.

I wish Ginnie a long life, but I am confident that people will be reading this book long after we are both gone. And they, like myself, will be thanking her for illuminating the path we must all follow, a path that society has festooned with needless fear, draped in anxiety, and spiced with gloom—the path of aging. In Virginia Bell's hands, that path is no longer so foreboding. Instead it beckons.

—Steven Forrest, author of *The Inner Sky*

ACKNOWLEDGMENTS

With Deep Appreciation

I am profoundly grateful to Mary Elizabeth Wakefield and Michel-Angelo for making the connection with Red Wheel/Weiser. I couldn't have found a better home for this book. It's been a joy working with Judika Illes, not only a superb editor but a kindred spirit. The entire Red Wheel/Weiser team has been both professional and kind—a rare combination! Thank you Michael Kerber, Jane Hagaman, Bonni Hamilton, Eryn Carter, Debra Woodward, Greg Brandenburgh, Tania Seymour, and a heartfelt thanks to Kathryn Sky-Peck.

A big karmic thank you to Ginny and Bob Duffy for driving me home from the Berkshires so many years ago and for Ginny reading Steven Forrest's book out loud. Steven Forrest, thank you for being such a generous teacher and friend and for the beautiful foreword. Ingrid Coffin and everyone at Blue Sky Ranch who are involved in producing Steven's Apprenticeship Program—you are the best!

I'm indebted to the extraordinary astrology teachers I've studied with: Wendy Ashley, Eileen McCabe, Anne Ortelee, Michael Lutin, and especially Shirley Soffer, who has been such an angel to this book. Amy Hertz and Susan Golomb were instrumental during the early stages of this project, as were Ronnie Grishman and *Dell Horoscope* magazine. I love being a part of *Watch!* magazine, and I am so grateful to everyone there.

Hadley Fitzgerald is not only a dear friend, but her expertise and wisdom throughout the writing of this book has been invaluable. I owe so much to photographer and website designer Irene Young for the stunning photographs, website, and blogs, not to mention the forty-plus year's friendship. I don't know what I would have done without Susan Kennedy, Kate Wechsler, and Judith Adler, whose support and friendship kept me sane. Thank you, Andrea Hanson, for the summers in Maine, the Arrowsic Writer's Retreat, and so much more; also Petra Hanson, Bret Cox, and Dali-da, for the Mill Valley haven.

Deep thanks to Karol Jackowski, Sally Davies, Christene Barberich, Sharon Hillman, Anne Hardy, Lisa Rosman, Hilda Giordano, Kate Rogovin, Janice Zwail, Joel Wechsler, Elizabeth Spring, Chris Zydel, Marvin Garriott, Joey Reiman (for your cosmic enthusiasm), and Lisa Zimmerman (for the late-night astrology talks and laughter). And to my dear family: my sister, Kate Bell; plus Hannah and Chris Sutton, Evan and Becca Gould, and Jordan Smith. I also thank Philip Lynn and Manny Wolf for always believing in me. A very special thanks to Brandy Gillmore for her treasured guidance. And last but not least, to all the wonderful clients I have had the privilege to work with. Thank you all from the bottom of my heart.

INTRODUCTION

I have to give Father Chase, my parish priest at St. Aloysius, credit for pushing me toward astrology, although he would be horrified if he knew. At fourteen, I was obsessed with the monthly *Dell Horoscope* magazine; not the in-depth articles, just the daily forecasts. I was miserable at home and wanted desperately to know if anything positive would happen to me.

I grew up in a wealthy Jewish community on the North Shore of Long Island; my parents were poor and Christian. My father worked as a short-order cook in an all-night diner; he was alcoholic and abusive. My mother was fragile and childlike and was slowly fading away; years later she would be diagnosed with schizophrenia. The magazine became my lifeline. Every month, I pored through the pages searching for some hope that I could grasp.

One day after Sunday school, I casually asked Father Chase his opinion of astrology. "The devil's work," he replied harshly, not missing a beat. I was shocked by his rigid attitude and closed mind. I knew almost nothing about astrology (apart from the fact that I was a Taurus), but I decided then and there to put my faith in the stars and not the saints. My fate was sealed.

I didn't immediately begin studying astrology after my encounter with Father Chase, but astrology seemed to follow me like a song on the radio that kept getting my attention. My next rendezvous with the stars was in the mid-sixties when I was living in Italy. I wanted to travel, be a film star, and live like Holly Golightly (the protagonist in *Breakfast at Tiffany's*), so I moved to Rome when I was nineteen. It was the early 1960s, and the film business in Rome had exploded; it was a time of Fellini's *La Dolce Vita,* Spaghetti Westerns, and big, splashy American coproductions. I found steady work, traveled all over the globe, and met fabulous people, but my career never really took off. I had a love/hate relationship with show business, with Rome, and with myself as well. At twenty-six, I didn't have a clue about who I was, what I wanted to do, or where I wanted to live.

A conversation over lunch with the great screenwriter Tullio Pinelli turned out to be life changing. One day, my dear friend, director Alberto Lattuada, invited me to lunch at his home. He and Signore Pinelli were collaborating on a film script. Over lunch, Signore Pinelli asked me about myself. I explained my dilemma; whether to remain in Rome and continue pursuing a career in film or return to New York. Signore Pinelli suggested I seek the advice of a group of alchemists who lived in Turin, the industrial city in the north of Italy. They were great seers whose work was the basis for the Federico Fellini film, *Juliet of the Spirits.* Signore Pinelli had grown up in Turin. It had been his idea for the film, and he was also one of the screen writers.

He provided me with a list of their names and phone numbers, and in a few days I was headed north on the Rapido (express train) to Turin with all my belongings. I decided that if these wise men told me to stay in Italy, I would return to Rome; if they advised me to leave, I would go on to New York. It wouldn't be the first time I put my fate in the hands of total strangers. Unfortunately, I forgot it was mid-August and the Italian holiday of *Ferragosto;* everyone in Italy goes on vacation, including alchemists. All except one, an astrologer named Doctor Arno—Italians love titles.

I was mesmerized by Doctor Arno, who sat behind a huge desk surrounded by piles of mysterious books. After consulting one of these enormous tomes, which I now know was an ephemeris, he assured me that I had extremely good luck (*molto fortuna*) in Europe, along with many other fascinating bits of information. I knew he was right about my luck, but something told me that I needed to return to the States. Although I didn't know it at the time, I was experiencing my Progressed Lunar Return, which precedes the Saturn Return—a period when our intuition is particularly strong. I decided to listen.

Back in New York, I could feel something within me shifting, and I knew it was time for me to get serious. That happens at the Saturn Return at age twenty-nine. It's as if we get a wake-up call, and we're finally ready to grow up, make a commitment, and take on more responsibility. For most of us, our late twenties and early thirties is a time to stop drifting and begin doing; we sober up— sometimes literally. We can't train forever; at some point, we have to step up to the starting line and begin the race. Saturn is that starting line. It is the first major cycle and the foundation for all the others.

I longed to do something, but what? I was obsessed with two things: exercise and health foods. I considered opening either an exercise studio or a natural foods restaurant. The food won; I'm a double Taurus—Sun and Moon in the sign of warm scones and crème fraiche.

In 1974, I opened one of the first gourmet natural foods restaurants in New York City. Naturally, I consulted an astrologer about an opening date. I had no experience and very little money, but I had a vision for the kind of food I wanted to create, plus something else that would prove indispensable: Saturn. I didn't know a Saturn Return from a tax return, but that's exactly what was going on. I made a commitment, worked really hard, and hung in there. The restaurant became a success, and I grew in the process.

Most of us spend our early to mid-thirties building something: a career, a family, or perhaps going back to school. What's important is that we commit to some task and work hard to make it happen. In the process, we gain stature, credentials, and experience. There may even be financial rewards and recognition. It can be a heady time; on our own and no longer tied to our families, we seem to have it all figured out. That is until around the age of thirty-seven.

Cracks appear in the structures we've carefully erected, and they begin to crumble. We're approaching forty, almost halfway through the average lifespan, which is a wake-up call. And while this cycle is commonly called a midlife crisis, and can certainly *feel* like one, it's really a mid-course correction. Whatever we've left out of the equation, whatever we've ignored, begins to rise up and can no longer be disregarded. This cycle involves four planets and is spread over a decade. Welcome to life's most important cycle.

I had been running the restaurant for about six years, and it was doing well. Thanks to glowing reviews in the *Village Voice* and *New York* magazine, customers were lining up around the block for the small planet casserole, our popular salad dressing, and the peanut butter ice cream pie. Plus, I was learning a lot, not just about the business and food but about people and myself. Then, in my late thirties, everything came crashing down. I thought I was having a nervous breakdown; instead, it was midlife. Who knew? My father died, and, as a result, I inherited the responsibility of taking care of my mother, who was mentally ill. At the very same time, I had problems in the restaurant and in my relationship. Basically, all my worst fears surfaced at once; I was raw, panicked, and in tremendous pain. It turned out to be a giant wake-up call. Not only did I survive, but my life and my business transformed in ways I never thought possible.

I had always been interested in psychology and had engaged in a lot of therapy. During the seventies and early eighties, I began exploring various spiritual paths, self-help seminars, and healing techniques. I did est (Erhard Seminars Training), Actualizations, studied yoga, discovered spirituality in Findhorn (in Northern Scotland), studied *A Course in Miracles,* and got in touch with my power by walking over hot coals with Tony Robbins. Although I didn't study astrology, it was never far away. I had an astrologer on staff at the restaurant; I fed him in exchange for readings. At the time, I thought of astrology only in terms of predictions and was always asking the same questions: When would the current crisis be over, or when would I meet my soulmate? I didn't realize it was deeper and more complex. But I was about to find out.

In my mid-forties, I decided to open another restaurant. Unfortunately, it was in the Berkshires in Western Massachusetts: the area was extremely seasonal—super busy in the summer but dead in the winter months. Not only did I lose a ton of money, the situation put pressure on the restaurant in Greenwich Village. Yet it was during this period that a friend, whom I met in the Berkshires, lent me a book by astrologer Steven Forrest entitled *The Inner Sky.* Steven's book brought astrology alive for me; his descriptions of the planets, signs, and houses were clear and accessible yet poetic and deeply meaningful. I began to see that astrology wasn't something merely happening in the sky but was within us as well and could be a valuable tool for self-discovery.

The Chiron Return takes place between ages forty-nine and fifty-one, when Chiron returns to its natal place. In mythology, Chiron was a great healer and teacher, and this passage is one of the best times to become fully conscious of whatever has not been healed. For many of us, our lives take off in a different direction from what we had anticipated, and often there is a failure or loss that serves as a catalyst for this.

I experienced plenty of both, including closing the restaurant in the Berkshires and then the one in New York City. The restaurant had been my identity for twenty years; without it, I didn't know who I was. An old life was ending, a terrifying thing—especially for a stubborn Taurus—but a new one was rising up from the ashes. I began studying astrology in my early fifties, not thinking of it as a career but simply because it gave me joy. But eventually, a career is exactly where it led.

At fifty-eight, we have our Second Saturn Return and enter the phase of the elder. Don't confuse elder with older; not everyone has the privilege of becoming an elder and embodying Saturn. Just as in our earlier Saturn Return, we need a great work, something that will define us in our elder years. For many, this third act is a period when life really comes together. I know that was true for me.

I was already doing astrology readings and writing Sun-sign columns for a couple of magazines. Then, in 2000, I joined Steven Forrest's apprenticeship program. Not only was it was an opportunity to study with a master astrologer, but also to learn about Evolutionary Astrology, which is the basis for the astrology that Steven teaches. Evolutionary Astrology is not simply another technique but also an approach that is based on responsibility, freedom of choice, and a respect for people's ability to grow. For me, it provided a spiritual framework, one that is holistic and soul centered, and became the basis for my own astrology practice.

The planet Uranus takes eighty-four years to come back to where it was at our birth. In our early sixties, it makes the last aspect before returning to its original position. The Uranus square is really a second wind; there's a sense of freedom that comes from this edgy aspect, provided we are willing to take some risks and extend ourselves beyond our comfort zone. It's worth doing, because the actions we take now will impact who we become at eighty-four when Uranus comes full circle.

By the time I was in my early sixties, I was well acquainted with the life cycles. I was approaching my final Uranus square and, given that change-at-all-cost Uranus was orchestrating this cycle, I knew I needed to take a big risk. For me, that meant selling my dearly loved house on Long Island. I did it, and it brought me the freedom I had been craving. It was in my early sixties that I began to notice something else: I finally began to feel good. I mean *really good*—happy, content, at peace. There were times when life wasn't challenging, and I felt good. But happy? It wasn't even on my radar. As I began to study aging, I saw that this wasn't unusual. Providing we are willing to do the inner work, these late-in-life transitions offer immense opportunities to grow, develop, and deepen.

There was something changing in me, but also in the world. The whole concept of aging and the second half of life were shifting: old walls were falling and new paradigms were emerging. In the not-so-distant past, aging was a taboo subject; senior citizens were shunned and excluded from mainstream society. But the tide is beginning to turn. With the youngest baby boomer just past fifty and the oldest in their seventies, there are simply too many to ignore. In the 1960s, we had the *youth quake*; now we're having the *age quake*. Like any movement, it's not perfect; but there is a new awareness, a bigger conversation, and a growing respect for people who are in the second half of life.

Simultaneously, astrology was having a renaissance. It has always been popular, but thanks to the Internet—with its websites, articles, and blogs, plus easy access to birth charts—its popularity has exploded. The idea of writing about the cycles and aging began to come together.

Looking back over my life, I wish I'd had a handbook for these great milestones and some instruction on how to negotiate them. Like any journey or excursion, it helps to have some knowledge of the terrain, so you can prepare and pack accordingly. There's an advantage to learning from others who have taken the voyage and returned with some wisdom as well as tales of setbacks and successes.

When I first went to Europe in 1962, the popular guidebook *Europe on 5 Dollars a Day* was my bible. I studied it endlessly on those long train rides across Europe; writing notes in the margins while making plans and plotting adventures. The book you hold in your hand is the guidebook I wish I'd had while traveling through the generational cycles. It offers information but also inspiration about each decade; how to prepare but also prosper, thrive, and evolve in the second half of life.

I look forward to you joining me on this journey. You don't need any prior knowledge of astrology, but I have included an overview of the basics. It comes with a warning: astrology is seductive and can become addictive. You will enter a magical realm, one filled with mythology, archetypes, and stories that can capture your imagination, open your mind, and shake up your beliefs. No bad side effects have been reported. Astrology is simply another lens through which to view the world.

INTRODUCTION TO THE CYCLES
Our Power Years

Just as there are power places in the world—sacred locations such as Glastonbury, Machu Pichu, and Sedona that are said to vibrate at a higher frequency and accelerate transformation—there are also power *years*. These years correspond to the generational or life cycles that we all share at the same ages:

* The Saturn Return at twenty-nine

* Midlife, which peaks at forty-two

* The Chiron Return, between forty-nine and fifty-one

* The Second Saturn Return at fifty-eight

* The Uranus square in our early sixties

* The Uranus conjunction at eighty-four

Transits are a method of prediction. They describe the movements of the planets overhead, and, like our transit systems here on Earth, they are always in motion. Because transits are linked to individual birth charts, they can occur at any time in our life. For instance, the planet Saturn can "make an aspect" (the relationship between one planet and another within the zodiac) to your Sun (or other planets in your chart) at any time. That is unique to your birth chart. When the planets arrive at a point in the sky that corresponds to a point in our chart, they generate an event, and something happens—this is the transit.

These power years or life cycles are determined by our age and shared with others born at the same time. These cycles take place when a planet makes an aspect to its own natal (birth) position. For instance, at age twenty-nine, Saturn *returns* to the place it occupied at birth; this is called the Saturn Return.

Just because many people experience these cycles at the same age doesn't make them less powerful or relevant. Think of those treasured rites of passage such as a Bar Mitzvah, Sweet Sixteen, or high school graduation: these events are imbued with meaning specifically because they are shared by so many and are deeply rooted in our culture. These rituals mark a person's progress from one stage to another. The generational cycles operate in the same way; they are the significant passages we all experience and that, strung together, tell the story of our lives.

We are all individuals with our own unique path, but on this journey called life, each and every one of us will come to certain crossroads or *cycles*. Although our fate may differ, the timing of these cycles is the same. These cycles or power years are the great turning points in life; at every juncture there will be challenges, lessons, and loses—in this we have no choice. Our freedom lies in how we respond: consciously or unconsciously, awake or asleep, with fear or with love. The planet that governs the cycle acts as a wise elder or guide and holds the key to navigating the cycle successfully and releasing the potential that lies within. This book is the story of these cycles. Ultimately, it describes the process of becoming whole.

A Brief History of the Cycles

These cycles are not confined to astrology; psychologists have been examining them for ages. Sigmund Freud (1856–1939) was the founder of psychoanalysis and, with the possible exception of William James, explored the human mind more than anyone who came before him. He laid the groundwork with his study of early childhood and how it influences one's life in adulthood. Carl Jung (1875–1961) made the greatest contribution to the study of adult development; he was the first psychologist to recognize midlife as a separate phase and the first to write about it extensively. He also coined the term "individuation" to describe the developmental process that begins at forty and extends throughout the second half of life. Erik H. Erikson (1902–1994) built on Jung's findings with his eight stages of life. In fact, his book *Childhood and Society* (1950) spawned a great deal of interest in the concept of the life cycles.

The late 1960s psychologist Daniel J. Levinson (1920–1994) gathered together a team and conducted a ten-year in-depth study of the adult life cycles. This study explored specific periods of personal development through which we all pass. He was building on the psychologists who had come before him, including his mentor, Else Frenkel-Brunswik (1908–1958), who was a pioneer in this field.

Journalist and author Gail Sheehy drew on these sources for her bestselling book, *Passages: Predictable Crises of Adult Life,* published in 1976. A superb writer and researcher, she was able to weave together psychology and sociology along with hundreds of interviews to create a clear map of the individual life cycles (through age fifty) that was both relevant and accessible. Her timing was impeccable: the late 1970s was a period of increasing self-discovery. People were waking up, and they needed to make sense of what they were experiencing. They recognized themselves in her themes: the trying twenties, the catch thirties, the forlorn forties, and the refreshed (or resigned) fifties.

There seems to be a kind of order in the universe, in the movement of the stars and the turning of the earth and the changing of the seasons, and even in the cycle of human life.
—Katherine Anne Porter

Astrologers have long been aware of these cycles, for they follow the same trajectory. Astrology may overlap with psychology at various times, but it is also distinct from therapy, counselling, or coaching—which are all extremely valuable. But astrology offers another perspective, one that is universal and tied in with cosmic awareness and a search for meaning.

Astrology, at its best, is a symbolic language and is therefore able to elude the cunning ego (so prone to judging and rejecting). It makes use of ancient archetypes, gods and goddesses of myth, as well as planets and stars that are much more exciting than those on reality shows. Although you may not be familiar with its technical language, references to astrology are everywhere: in poetry, Shakespeare's plays, art, song, books, movies—indeed every time we marvel at the heavens above and sing its praises. We experience astrology's connection in the passing seasons and nightly when we watch the moon. Knowledge of astrology's cycles gives us valuable guidance for navigating these great passages that we all share.

AN OVERVIEW OF ASTROLOGY
The Birth Chart

To paraphrase Carl Jung: Anything born at a moment in time has the characteristics of that moment. The birth chart is a picture of the sky at the moment of birth. It is a snapshot of the heavens and all the planets. It is frozen in time. In the next moment, everything moves, but that picture is yours forever; it is eternal, a piece of cosmic DNA.

> *We're born, and from that moment we carry inside ourselves a little hologram of the sky. As long as we live, it resonates with the rhythms of the planets and tides, stars and seasons. That hologram is our life; its breath is the breathing of an intelligent, conscious universe. Studying that hologram is the delicate, ever changing art we call astrology.[1]*
> —Steven Forrest

I like to compare the birth chart to those little packets of seeds that arrive in the mail every spring. Inside the packet are the seeds,

---

[1]Steven Forrest, *The Night Speaks: A Meditation on the Astrological Worldview* (San Diego: ACS Publications, 1993), pp. 7–8.

and on the outside is a brightly colored picture of the flower. The packet comes with instructions about the kind of soil the seeds require, as well as how much sunlight and water is needed. There is no guarantee that the seeds will flower to look like the picture on the front of the packet, but it has the potential; with the proper care, it can flourish.

We, too, come with instructions; that's the birth chart. It tells us what we need to stay healthy and happy; it describes our strengths, gifts, and goals and how best to actualize them. It also describes our weaknesses and vulnerabilities and how to heal. Nothing is preordained; we must participate with the process. The birth chart is merely potential, and, like the picture of the flower on the seed packet, it shows us what we look like when we get it right.

> *Astrology is astronomy brought down*
> *to earth and applied to the affairs of men.*
> —Ralph Waldo Emerson

The Language of Astrology

Astrology is a language, so it helps to known some of the vocabulary. In astrology, there's an enormous amount of information, but there are three main concepts or functions, and if you have a working knowledge of these, you are on your way to understanding how to "speak" astrology. The three concepts are: *planets, signs,* and *houses.*

The Planets

They are the *verb, the action;* without the planets, there would be no astrology. Think of them as the actors in a play; they move the story along. The word "planet" comes from the Greek and means "wanderer." They are the Sun, Moon, and eight other planets. Although the Sun and Moon are not technically planets, these large planetary bodies are all grouped together to make it easier. The eight planets are Mercury, Venus, Mars, Jupiter, Saturn, Uranus, Neptune, and Pluto. Chiron is in a category by itself; although it is a minor planet, it's a significant one, as it plays a major role in the generational cycles. The planets represent different energies within us; they also represent the people in our lives. For instance, the Moon represents our mother, but it's also how we "mother" ourselves, what nurtures and comforts us. Each planet has an agenda, a voice, and a role to play.

In 2006, astronomers "demoted" Pluto to a dwarf planet, but most astrologers agree that Pluto is too powerful to dismiss. At the same time, Ceres (an asteroid) was *elevated* to the status of a dwarf planet. There have also been new planets discovered such as Sedna and Eris. Are you still with me? As astrologers learn more about the new planets, they will be able to incorporate them in the chart. For our purpose, we will stay with those mentioned above.

The Signs

If each planet is an actor in the play, then the signs are how the actors express themselves; signs demonstrate *styles of behavior.* The Moon is always the Moon (our heart, our feelings, and intuition), but it behaves differently in tender Cancer than it does in feisty Aries. Think of the signs as how the actors in the play communicate and conduct themselves. There are twelve signs: Aries, Taurus, Gemini, Cancer, Leo, Virgo, Libra, Scorpio, Sagittarius, Capricorn, Aquarius, and Pisces. Each sign contains tools, resources, strengths, and talents, as well as limitations and shortcomings.

The Houses

The houses are the twelve slices of pie in the circle that represents the chart: six below the horizon and six above. They tell us *where* the action takes place. If the planets are the actors and the signs are how the actors express themselves, then the houses represent the stage (or the arena) on which the action unfolds. Each house describes a different area of your life.

A Family of Symbols

There is a planet, sign, and house that are all *related;* they belong to the same family. They are not interchangeable, but they are connected. For instance, the seventh house is the natural home of

Libra (the seventh sign), and Libra is ruled by the planet Venus. All three are associated with love, beauty, values, and committed relationships. The sign Cancer (the fourth sign) is associated with the fourth house and the Moon; all three relate to home, family, and nurturing.

The Planets

The Sun and Moon are referred to as luminaries because they are the brightest objects in the heavens and the most influential.

The Sun

The sun is new each day.
— Heraclitus

The life-giving Sun in the sky is the gravitational center of the solar system; it's what holds everything together. On a psychological level, the Sun is what holds *us* together. It is the most important component in the birth chart and relates to our sanity and our authenticity as a person. It is our identity, our ego, our will to live, and our ability to act. We must be true to our Sun if we're going to be real.

The sign that our Sun is in tells us what we need so as to stay healthy and sane. It also represents our father, the men in our life, and authority figures. The Sun rules the sign Leo and the fifth house.

The Moon

Moonlight drowns out all but the brightest stars.
—J. R. R. Tolkien

We all have a relationship with the Moon. Who hasn't stood outside on a clear night and gazed up in awe at a luminous full Moon?

Watching it is an emotional experience. In astrology, the Moon relates to our emotions; it correlates to our inner life. The Sun acts; the Moon receives. The Moon is our heart, our soul, our feelings, desires, and intuition. Just as taking care of the Sun ensures our sanity, by taking care of our Moon, we guarantee our happiness. The Moon also relates to our home, our mother, and the women in our life. It rules the sign Cancer and the fourth house.

The Inner or Personal Planets

The inner or personal planets move quickly through the zodiac and describe our inner, subjective life, our day-to-day world.

MERCURY
You can't learn less.
—Buckminster Fuller

Mercury moves faster than any other planet, not unlike our thoughts and speech, which it represents. Mercury is the planet of information, communication, teaching, and early education. It describes our mental style, how we express ourselves, and how we learn. Mercury also governs transportation and short trips. In Roman mythology, Mercury (the Greek Hermes) was a multi-tasker who was known as the messenger of the gods; he also ruled crossroads, travelers, and transactions. Mercury rules two signs and two houses: Gemini and the third house, as well as Virgo and the sixth house.

VENUS
Love comforteth like sunshine after rain.
—Shakespeare, "Venus and Adonis"

Venus is the brightest and whitest of planets; it is the nearest planet to Earth, and, because it is so visible, we naturally feel close to it.

In Greek mythology, it is associated with Aphrodite, the goddess of love and beauty (the Roman Venus). Venus rules socialization, partnership, and courtship. Venus represents the need for harmony and balance in relationships, nature, and art. Venus tells us what we are attracted to and how we draw it to us. It has dominion over two signs and two houses: Taurus and the second house, as well as Libra and the seventh house.

MARS

Life is either a daring adventure or nothing.
—Helen Keller

Red-hot Mars is associated with the Roman god of war; it represents conflict and aggression but also courage, will, passion, and independence. Mars is our engine; it's what drives us. It is the planet of survival, self-interest, and the striving for personal power. If Venus describes how we attract love, Mars tells how to pursue it. In Greek mythology, Mars is identified with the god Ares, who had a secret love affair with Aphrodite (Venus). Mars is the ancient ruler of Scorpio and the eighth house, and the modern ruler of Aries and the first house.

The Social Planets

The social planets don't move as quickly as the personal planets, so they are less subjective; but they are not as slow (or distant) as the outer ones. They describe how we relate within the framework of society and the times in which we are born.

JUPITER

Nothing great was ever achieved without enthusiasm.
—Ralph Waldo Emerson

Jupiter is the biggest planet, and it represents expansion, abundance, faith, generosity, and prosperity. It is the archetype of the king, Santa Claus, and the proverbial rich uncle. Jupiter protects and looks after us in whatever sign and house it is in. Traditionally, it is a "lucky" planet, although go-for-broke Jupiter is also associated with overindulgence and overextension. In Roman mythology, Jupiter (the Greek Zeus) was king of the gods. Jupiter is an ancient ruler of Pisces and the twelfth house, and the modern ruler of Sagittarius and the ninth house.

SATURN
Don't ask for a lighter load; ask for a stronger back.
—author unknown

Saturn (known as Cronus to the Greeks) is the slowest of the classical planets (those easily seen by the naked eye); where Saturn is in our chart indicates where we tend to be slow, cautious, and somewhat fearful. The ringed planet represents limitations, barriers, and boundaries. Saturn has a reputation for being difficult, but its purpose is to help us mature. It takes time to learn these lessons, which is why Saturn improves with age. Saturn is the ancient ruler of Aquarius and the eleventh house, and the modern ruler of Capricorn and the tenth house.

The Outer or Invisible Planets

For thousands of years, humanity knew seven planets—including the Sun and Moon—as these were the only planets visible to the naked eye. Saturn, the most distant of them, stood guard at the edge of the solar system. That was before telescopes . . .

In 1781, astronomer William Herschel, using a telescope, discovered Uranus—and the world broke open. In 1846, Neptune was discovered and then in 1930, Pluto. These so-called "outer planets" travel slowly, remain in a sign for many years, and leave their mark on an entire generation.

The outer planets are the "transpersonal" ones, which are concerned with energies beyond the self: the collective, the big picture, the zeitgeist. When two of these planets come together in the sky, such as Uranus and Pluto did in the mid-sixties, there is revolution, upheaval, and transformation.

URANUS
Expect the unexpected.
—conventional wisdom

Named after the Greek sky god, Uranus is the associated with anything innovative, unpredictable, and original. It rules astrology, technology, intellectual brilliance, and esoteric knowledge. This planet of surprises moves slowly, but when it makes contact with another planet, it has the power to disrupt the natural flow of events.

We're not all rebels, but where we find Uranus in our charts is where we want to break free, challenge authority, and think for ourselves. For instance, if we have Uranus in our seventh house of one-to-one relationships, we would require freedom in a relationship, have nontraditional relationships, or be attracted to people who are unconventional. Uranus rules the sign Aquarius and the eleventh house.

NEPTUNE
Imagination is more important than knowledge.
—Albert Einstein

Named after the mythic Roman god of the sea, and known to the Greeks as Poseidon, Neptune is the planet of the invisible and unseen. It rules those things that cannot be seen with the naked eye, such as inspiration, imagination, music, and spirituality, as well as escapism and addiction. Neptune rules Pisces and the twelfth house. Where we have Neptune in our chart is where we seek to merge, to sacrifice, and to relinquish our ego.

PLUTO
There are higher things than the ego's will, and to these one must bow.
—Carl Jung

Pluto may be small in size, but its power is immense. In Greek mythology, Pluto was Hades, the god of the underworld, feared by mortals and by the other gods. The planet Pluto represents all those things that frightens us: death, aging, intimacy, mysticism. It is our fundamental wound, our Shadow; it is where we die to be reborn. Pluto digs deeply; therefore, it is associated with research, depth psychology, surgery, and transformation. Pluto rules Scorpio and the eight house.

Bridge Planet
CHIRON
*The practice of forgiveness is our most important
contribution to the healing of the world.*
—Marianne Williamson

Chiron is a minor planet that was discovered in 1977, around the time that the word "healing" entered the language and the New Age movement was burgeoning. In Greek mythology, Chiron was a centaur—born half man, half horse—who became a great teacher, beloved for his compassion. Often described as the "wounded healer," Chiron is associated with healing, forgiveness, and ecology. Where we have Chiron in our chart is where we have a wound but also the ability to heal.

Signs

Every sign has a high expression—who we are when we're operating at our best—as well as a dark side or Shadow. The Shadow is not a prediction; it's merely on the opposite end of the spectrum and describes what happens should we fail to live up to our potential.

Dates are approximate, depending on each calendar year. The Sun always moves at different speeds, so the date the Sun enters a sign can change from year to year—but it is always around the same date. For instance, the Sun enters Aries around March 20 or 21. If someone is born on the cusp (on or between the possible dates), the only way to know the correct sign is to have a chart calculated. (This can be done for free online. Just Google "free astrology chart.")

Aries (the Ram): March 21–April 19

Aries, a fire sign, is ruled by action-planet Mars. Arriving on the first day of spring, Aries is the first sign and therefore the "baby" of the zodiac. As a result, Arians possess qualities of energy and youthful *naïveté,* which they never lose. They believe they can do anything and often succeed. They are the leaders, pioneers, and daredevils; they forge ahead with a confidence that's contagious.

> **Shadow:** They have a short fuse and can get sidetracked by petty arguments and skirmishes. They are great initiators but sometimes don't follow through.

> **Well-known Aries:** Thomas Jefferson, Vincent van Gogh, Marlon Brando, Jane Goodall, Sarah Jessica Parker, Lady Gaga

Taurus (the Bull): April 20–May 20

Taurus is the first earth sign. Ruled by elegant Venus, Taureans have refined taste, but they are remarkably down to earth. They have a strong need for comfort, security, and natural surroundings. A sensual sign, Taurus is nourished by taste, texture, color, music, and delicious food. Taurus could be in the dictionary next to the word "cozy."

> **Shadow:** They love their naps, their snacks, and little luxuries. They prefer safety over surprises and can be stubborn and slow to change.
>
> **Well-known Taureans:** Leonardo da Vinci, Audrey Hepburn, Queen Elizabeth II, Adele, Bono, George Clooney

Gemini (the Twins): May 21–June 20

Gemini, the first air sign, is ruled by multitasking Mercury. Geminis love being busy and hate being bored; they are here to live five lifetimes in one. They are master communicators, media experts, and teachers and thrive on information, stimulation, and change. It's not unusual for them to have two jobs, two homes, even two separate personalities. Their minds work overtime, so they are susceptible to insomnia and nerves.

> **Shadow:** They can become frazzled and buried in details. They can talk about anything except their own feelings.
>
> **Well-known Geminis:** Ralph Waldo Emerson, John F. Kennedy, Marilyn Monroe, Paul McCartney, Angelina Jolie, Donald Trump

Cancer (the Crab): June 21–July 22

Cancer, a water sign ruled by the Moon, is motivated by emotions rather than logic, which makes them deep, sensitive, compassionate, and intuitive. Cancers love home, food, and family. Like their symbol, the crab, they need a cozy refuge to which they can retreat, as well as something or someone to nurture and lots of downtime. They are the mothers, fathers, and healers of the zodiac.

> **Shadow:** Their flaws are their claws; they tend to hang on to memories, relationships, and objects. Cancers can also be moody. They may hide behind the role of the nurturer, taking care of everyone but themselves.

> **Well-known Cancers:** Frida Kahlo, Princess Diana, the Dalai Lama, Nelson Mandela, Giorgio Armani, Tom Hanks

Leo (the Lion): July 23–August 22

Leo, the second fire sign, represents the lion—the king, the queen, and the performer. Ruled by the mighty Sun, Leos are here to shine; although at their core, they are shy. Saying "yes" to life is their mantra. They are learning to trust life and to know that you cannot express yourself unless you reveal yourself. Creativity, children, and romance feed their souls.

> **Shadow:** Their pride is their Achilles heel and can cause them to crash and burn if they're not conscious of it.

> **Well-known Leos:** Coco Chanel, Carl Jung, Mick Jagger, Madonna, Martha Stewart, Barack Obama

Virgo (the Virgin): August 23–September 22

Virgo, an Earth sign, is ruled by Mercury; it is the sign of work, health, service, and craftsmanship. Finding a work or craft they love, perfecting it, polishing it, and offering it to the world is the Virgo's Holy Grail. They are often drawn to health and healing professions and are committed to making the world a better place.

> **Shadow:** No one works harder on themselves than Virgo, but they can also be extremely critical of themselves—and others! Virgos need to learn to love themselves for who they are and not just for what they do.

> **Well-known Virgos:** Mother Teresa, Greta Garbo, Stephen King, Sean Connery, Sophia Loren, Prince Harry

Libra (the Scales): September 23–October 22

Libra, an air sign, is ruled by beautiful Venus, the goddess of love; it is the sign of marriage and partnership. Librans fare better being in a relationship than going it alone. They have the gift of creating rapport with others and are master counselors, diplomats, and negotiators. They are extremely sensitive to harmony and require a calm and peaceful environment to thrive.

> **Shadow:** Libras can be passive aggressive: keeping harmony at all cost, avoiding confrontation, and being codependent.

> **Well-known Librans:** John Lennon, Mahatma Gandhi, Jimmy Carter, Sting, Kim Kardashian, Barbara Walters

Scorpio (the Scorpion): October 23–November 21

Scorpio, a water sign, has a reputation for being sexy, mysterious, and dangerous, but it's really about intensity. It's not uncommon for Scorpios to have experienced some loss early in life and for them to live more passionately as a result. Ruled by Pluto, lord of the underworld and the planet of transformation, Scorpios love delving deeply into things and are drawn to the taboo. They are the shamans, psychologists, politicians, bankers, and detectives of the zodiac.

> **Shadow:** Scorpios may have too much self-knowledge or too little and an addiction to drama and to repeating old, wounding scenarios.

> **Well-known Scorpios:** Pablo Picasso, Georgia O'Keeffe, Indira Gandhi, Bill Gates, Leonardo DiCaprio, Hillary Clinton

Sagittarius (the Archer): November 22–December 21

Sagittarius, another fire sign, is the sign of the quest; they may not know the meaning of life, but they know life has meaning, and they are on a quest to find it. Travel, philosophy, and higher learning are all essential to their journey. They crave freedom and the open road. Ruled by giant Jupiter, Sagittarians possess deep faith, confidence, enthusiasm, and a generous spirit. They have the ability to inspire us with what inspires them.

> **Shadow:** Sagittarians are prone to overextension, exaggeration, and black-and-white thinking.

Well-known Sagittarians: Walt Disney, Frank Sinatra, Emily Dickinson, Tina Turner, Steven Spielberg, Keith Richards

Capricorn (the Sea-Goat): December 22–January 19

Capricorn, an earth sign ruled by Saturn, is serious, ambitious, and goal driven. It's not merely about a day-to-day job; they need a *calling, a mission;* work they can do in the world that expresses who they are inside. This sign is often associated with business and banking, but there are Capricorns in every field. They bring excellence and integrity to whatever they focus upon. They are late bloomers; Capricorns are born old and get younger as they age.

> **Shadow:** Capricorns tend to isolate themselves, control their feelings, and seek approval through their public roles rather than their inner worth.

> **Well-known Capricorns:** Martin Luther King Jr., Henri Matisse, Paramahansa Yogananda, Richard Nixon, Michelle Obama, Kate Middleton

Aquarius (the Water-Bearer): January 20–February 18

The final air sign is free-thinking Aquarius; those born under this sign are the rebels, the eccentrics, and the geniuses of the zodiac. Ruled by unconventional Uranus, they're here to bring something new and original to the world. In order to do that, they must break some rules and challenge the status quo. They need a cause they can believe in, a group of like-minded people, and lots of freedom.

Shadow: If they lack a genuine cause to defend, Aquarians may fight *against* something (rather than for it) and run the risk of losing themselves in the process.

Well-known Aquarians: Thomas Edison, Jackson Pollock, Virginia Woolf, Bob Marley, Sarah Palin, Oprah Winfrey

Pisces (the Fish): February 19–March 20

Pisces, a water sign, is the sign of the dreamer, the mystic, the artist, and the musician. Ruled by Neptune, mythic god of the sea, Pisceans are in touch with the invisible world. They feel everything deeply, which makes them highly sensitive, caring, compassionate, and romantic. They need periods of quiet and meditation and are at their best near water.

Shadow: Pisceans are vulnerable to escapism, addiction, and becoming the martyr. When overwhelmed, they tend to create obsessions rather than make decisions.

Well-known Pisceans: Albert Einstein, Frédéric Chopin, Michelangelo, Elizabeth Taylor, Steve Jobs, Cindy Crawford

Houses

Each house correlates to a different sign. The planet that rules that sign is called its *natural* ruler. For example, the first house is associated with Aries, which is the first sign. Thus Mars, the ruler of Aries, is the natural ruler of the first house—for everyone, regardless of their Sun sign. Aries and Mars have dominion over the first house. Any planet found in that house will behave like an Aries—even a

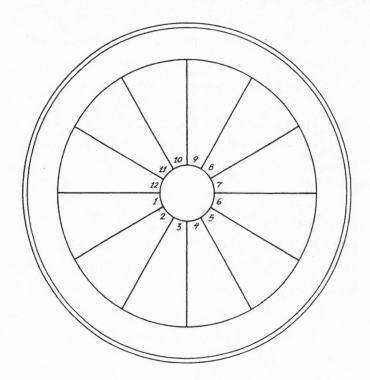

dreamy Pisces, whose Sun falls in the first house, will be more self-motivated and proactive (typical of Aries) than the average Pisces.

Think of the natural ruler as a sovereign. When England ruled India, the people were accountable to the sovereign and took on many of the qualities and customs of the English, although they were still Indian and had their own language, religion, and culture.

The "cusp" is the dividing line between each house, the entrance to the house, the doorway. The sign on the cusp of the house has its own ruler. For instance, if Scorpio is on a cusp, then Pluto rules that house. The planet that rules that house is like a landlord; he's the one holding the lease and calling the shots. The planet *living* in the house is the tenant and thus beholden to the ruler. In order to learn this information, you must have your chart done, whether by an astrologer or through one of the many astrology sites on the Internet.

Empty Houses

All of our charts have houses that are devoid of planets. There are twelve houses but only ten planets, plus Chiron. Think of it this way: in school we all take math, but not all of us become accountants. We each have our own areas of focus. Essentially, we are all majoring in something; the location of a concentration of planets in your chart indicates what you are majoring in during this lifetime.

Oprah doesn't have a strong career house. She's an Aquarius, and she's here to change the world—that's her major.

Although a house may lack planets, that doesn't mean that it lacks energy. As previously mentioned, the actual sign on the house cusp—the *beginning* of the house—has a ruling planet; the sign and location of that planet in the chart tells a story.

First House: Me first!

The first house, which is associated with Aries and Mars, represents action, courage, and willpower. The first house is our identity, ego, and persona. This is the house of the ascendant (your rising sign), your personality and personal style.

People with the Sun in the first house (like Freddie Mercury, Brad Pitt, and the Dalai Lama) are charismatic and bigger than life. They also tend to be self-made. Any planet in the first house is visible and contributes to our individual style, appearance, and mannerisms. For instance, Bill Clinton has Venus, Mars, and Neptune all in pleasing Libra in the first house, and he radiates charm.

Second House: Money makes the world go around.

The second house is associated with Taurus, the second sign, and its ruler, Venus. This house has to do with money, values, resources, talents, and self-esteem.

Money will be a significant theme for those with their Sun in the second house—they are learning about possessions, property, and earning power. Ultimately, it's not about acquiring wealth; *it's about building self-worth.* Oprah Winfrey is a great example. She has become a billionaire, but along the way, she has dealt with a lot of self-esteem issues and is teaching us all to "Live your best life now."

Third House: Knowledge is power.

The third house is connected to Gemini, the third sign, and its ruler, Mercury. This house is associated with communication, information, learning, as well as with siblings, early childhood, our immediate environment, and short trips.

People with a strong third house are natural writers, teachers, and storytellers. They are always on the move and are superb networkers, bringing projects and people together. Like Bono (whose Taurus Sun falls in the third house), they are master wordsmiths who juggle many talents and interests.

Fourth House: Home is where the heart is.

The fourth house is the natural domain of Cancer and the Moon. The emphasis here is on home, family, and roots. It is our literal home, as well as "where we come from"; our foundation, heritage, and our personal myth.

People born with the Sun here are often associated with their place of birth. Bruce Springsteen's Libra Sun resides in the fourth house. He is deeply loyal to his home state of New Jersey; he writes songs about it, sings about it, and still lives there. Those born with their Sun in the fourth house tend to be deep thinkers.

Fifth House: There's no business like show business. (Irving Berlin)

The fifth house is the natural house of Leo and its ruler, the Sun. It represents creativity, self-expression, children, love affairs, pleasure, and sports.

People with planets in the fifth house are here to express themselves and have a powerful need to create and perform. Like the sign Leo, they need to shine and to get the world to clap for them. Mozart, Leonardo da Vinci, and Dolly Parton were all born with their Sun in the fifth house.

Sixth House: How may I serve you?

The natural home of Virgo and Mercury, the sixth house is associated with health, work, service, daily routines, and craftsmanship.

Finding work they love that is also useful to others is essential to those with planets here. Many sixth house people work in health-related fields (acupuncturists, therapists, healers), teach, or do volunteer work. A number of musicians, such as John Lennon and Michael Jackson, have their Sun in this house. Steven Spielberg and Robert Redford have their Sun in the sixth house, and each make socially conscious films.

Seventh House: It takes two to tango.

Libra and Venus are the natural rulers of the seventh house, also known as the "House of Marriage." It is associated with partnerships, art, and beauty.

Anyone whose Sun is here is an honorary Libra; they do better when working with people than when alone. This includes marriage partners but also any important one-to-one relationships, such as close friends or business partners. Many therapists, such as Sigmund

Freud, have their Sun in this house. Many artists and performers have planets here as well, such as Lady Gaga and Chris Martin.

Eighth House: Go to the places that scare you. (Pema Chodron)

The eighth house, the natural home of Scorpio and its ruling planet Pluto, is also known as "The House of Death." This house is associated with all the taboo subjects that frighten us: intimacy, taxes, other people's money, the afterlife, and the occult.

Having your Sun in the eighth doesn't mean you'll die early—eighth house folks are survivors—but like Shirley MacLaine and James Van Praagh, you might be drawn to psychic phenomena and reincarnation. You might even make a lot of money from it. Eighth house folk are the shamans, healers, and hospice workers of the zodiac; willing to go where most people won't tread.

Ninth House: The road is better than the inn. (Miguel de Cervantes)

The ninth house is the natural home of Sagittarius and Jupiter. Medieval astrologers called it the "House of Long Journeys over Water," and it is associated with travel and foreigners. It's also connected to journeys of the mind, philosophy, religion, higher learning, publishing, the law, and big ideas.

Those born with a strong ninth house influence—such as the great American writer Henry Miller, whose Sun is in this house, and Angelina Jolie, whose Moon is here—often live and work abroad or speak foreign languages. Jackie Kennedy Onassis had her Sun here, and she spent time abroad and spoke fluent French.

Tenth House: I am here to live out loud. (Emile Zola)

The tenth is the house of destiny, career, honor, and reputation. It is the natural home of goal-oriented Capricorn, and its ruling planet is Saturn. Planets located in this house, as well as the sign on the house cusp, offer valuable clues about vocation and direction in life.

People born with their Sun here need more than a job; they need a calling, a mission. Some folks born with their Sun in the tenth house, such as Albert Einstein, Bernie Sanders, Martha Stewart, and Jack Nicholson, have big careers and live in the public eye.

Eleventh House: You've got a friend. (Carole King)

The eleventh house, the natural home of Aquarius and the planet Uranus, has to do with friends, groups, and organizations.

Folks born with the Sun here resemble Aquarians; they are socially conscious, want to change the world, and are great networkers. Examples include many politicians, such as Bill Clinton, who was born with his Leo in the eleventh house, as well as people who attract followers via social media, such as Kim Kardashian. Planets located in the eleventh house behave like time-release vitamins; their influence becomes stronger over time. Many people born with their Sun in this house are late bloomers.

Twelfth House: To believe in God is to know that all the rules are fair, and that there will be wonderful surprises. (Ugo Betti)

The twelfth house is associated with the sign Pisces and its ruling planet, Neptune. Medieval astrologers called it the "House of Trouble," yet it is the most spiritual of the houses. How can that be? Well, if you don't have some kind of spiritual path, then you're in trouble.

Mahatma Gandhi, Johnny Cash, and Madonna were all born with the Sun in the twelfth house, and they all found their way to God. The real work of the twelfth house is inner work. People born with their Sun in this house tend to be sensitive, intuitive, and highly impressionable. They require regular periods of solitude and quiet.

The Ascendant

There is nothing that gives more assurance than a mask.
—Colette

We know what planets are in which house because of the time of one's birth; the time sets the horoscope. The word "horoscope" comes from the Greek word *horoskopos,* which means "I watch the hour."

In astrology, directions are reversed—"east" is found on the left of the chart. The sign on the eastern horizon is known as the *ascendant* or *rising sign.* This is the sign that was rising at dawn at the moment of birth—it is literally how we *dawn* on people. The ascendant describes our physical appearance, our style, or our *brand.* It's the mask that we wear in the world. It's not what's inside the package but rather how the package is wrapped.

That may sound superficial, but it isn't; we all need a style to help us navigate through life. The ascendant is your backstage pass, your ticket into certain parties and clubs; it opens doors. Getting your ascendant right allows you to express yourself comfortably in the world.

The ascendant is what people notice first—the impression that you make, your handshake, your hair; it's how you meet the world. Marilyn Monroe was a Gemini; she was a lot more intelligent than many people probably realized. What we saw was her rising sign, Leo—the lion's mane, the noble carriage, and the dazzling presence.

On the other hand, Mick Jagger is a Leo with Gemini rising, ruled by Mercury. His style is mercurial, agile, and electric. His face may have some wear and tear, but he still "moves like Jagger."

> **The Ruler of the Ascendant:** The planet that rules the ascendant (the first house) is the boss of the chart and gains importance as a result. The position of the ruling planet signifies your primary energy and the area of life that motivates you to act.

Rising Signs (Ascendants)

Aries: Aries wears the mask of the warrior, the daredevil, and the hero. Ruled by Mars, Aries have one speed, and it's fast; they charge through life. They like making the decisions and running the show. Their style is pushy and impatient, but they're really like a big, friendly golden retriever that means no harm. You don't live *with* them; you live *around* them. (Examples: James Dean, Joan Rivers, Stevie Nicks, Rihanna)

Taurus: Taurus rising wears the mask of the Earth Mother/Father. These people appear easygoing and laid back. Ruled by Venus, they also often exhibit grace and beauty. They are unpretentious and solidly in their bodies. Those born with Taurus rising have tremendous stamina and staying power but move at their own pace. (Examples: Henry Fonda, Humphrey Bogart, Serena Williams, Halle Berry, Mariah Carey)

Gemini: Gemini rising wears the mask of the storyteller, media maven, student, writer, and communicator. Curious and speedy, those born with this ascendant know how to adapt and think on their feet. Their style is youthful, slender, graceful, and social. They communicate easily; getting to know them is harder. (Examples: Voltaire, Amy Winehouse, J. K. Rowling, Mick Jagger, Matthew McConaughey)

Cancer: Ruled by the Moon, Cancer rising carries the archetype of the mother, father, healer, nurturer. Those born with this ascendant want to take care of the whole world, but they often ignore their own needs. They are deeply caring and compassionate people but also moody, cautious, and private. They respond to things emotionally rather than mentally. (Examples: Judy Garland, Steven Spielberg, the Dalai Lama, Bill Gates, Angelina Jolie)

Leo: You know when someone with Leo rising walks into a room; they project a sunny, confident persona and typically have excellent posture. They like to be treated as royalty and radiate a quality of old money. Male or female, you can't help noticing their hair. (Examples: Marilyn Monroe, Tina Turner, Johnny Depp, Jennifer Lopez, Donald Trump)

Virgo: Virgo rising appears helpful, responsible, and hardworking; they give you the sense that you can depend on them. Ruled by Mercury, the bachelor god, those born with this rising sign remain youthful. They generally have wiry bodies, are slender, and have regular, even features. They prefer solid colors and clean, simple lines. (Examples: Walt Disney, Roger Federer, Tom Ford, Jay Z, Steve Jobs)

Libra: Libra rising, ruled by Venus, wears the mask of the lover, the peacemaker, and the diplomat. Those born with this ascendant have the ability to connect with a wide range of people. Their looks are pleasing, even beautiful; their persona is charming and gracious. They exhibit good taste, dress well, and have a strong sense of color and style. There's a tendency to be all things to all people and to become invisible in the process. (Examples: Jimmy Carter, Bill Clinton, Barbara Walters, Kate Middleton, Jennifer Aniston)

Scorpio: Scorpio rising radiates that "don't mess with me" attitude. They often have sexy "bedroom eyes," hidden behind big sunglasses—they are intensely private—and often dress in black. They seem to know everything about you, but you rarely know anything about them, and that's the way they like it. The unenlightened are prone to manipulate; the evolved ones are true healers and shamans. (Examples: Sigmund Freud, Keith Richards, Gloria Steinem, Beyoncé, Vladimir Putin)

Sagittarius: Sagittarius wears the mask of the gypsy, the pilgrim, and the philosopher; their style is colorful, exotic, high spirited, and enthusiastic. There is something of the cowboy or cowgirl in them; edgy, outspoken, and willing to take risks. Those born with this rising sign are natural teachers, coaches, and motivators. They hide their problems behind their easy humor and cheerful demeanor. (Examples: Elvis Presley, Nelson Mandela, Ted Turner, Oprah Winfrey, Brad Pitt)

Capricorn: One word about this rising sign: *gravitas.* Those born with this ascendant radiate dignity, seriousness, and authority and have a great presence. They set out to build a life and a career in an orderly fashion. They often have a lot of responsibility early in life, which makes them seem older than their years. It's not easy for these people to show their feelings; they often appear reserved.

(Examples: Queen Elizabeth II, Sophia Loren, Sean Connery, Catherine Deneuve, Bono)

Aquarius: Aquarius rising comes across as the rebel, the genius, and the nonconformist. There is often something unconventional and magnetic about the way they look or dress. Although they seem quite forward thinking, they may be intolerant of others' opinions and ideas. (Examples: Abraham Lincoln, Carl Jung, Janis Joplin, Jim Morrison, David Bowie)

Pisces: Pisces rising wears the mask of the artist, the musician, the poet, and the dreamer. Their style tends to be soft, gentle, sexy but nonthreatening. Like water, they seem to flow with whatever is happening and leave the decision-making to others. Look for mussed up hair and that "come hither stare." (Examples: Antonio Banderas, George Clooney, Jimmy Fallon, Gwyneth Paltrow, Deepak Chopra)

The Nodes of the Moon

The nodes of the Moon relate the birth chart to history; where we were before this life and where we are headed in this one. There are two nodes, and they are always opposite each other, 180 degrees apart; they exist in tension.

The South Node: The South Node symbolizes our karmic past. It represents the life we lived before this one, with all its problems and perplexities. (If you are not comfortable with the concept of past lives, then think of the South Node as representing your heritage or early childhood.) We are drawn back there, because it is familiar and comfortable but not necessarily healthy.

The North Node: The North Node represents the evolutionary future to which we are heading. It always feels unfamiliar, and something in us tries to reject it. Yet it is our North Node that contains our health and sanity.

Think of the South Node as the junk food and the North Node as the gym.

* The South Node is where we are addicted, obsessed, and unreasonable; been there, smoked that, and so forth.

* The North Node is like joining the gym or giving up smoking; it takes us forever to finally do it, but once we do, it's such a relief because it feels so right.

Like planets, the nodes occupy a sign and a house. Understanding the nodes, along with the karmic story that they represent, can help us understand our past drama so that we may live more fully in the present.

Aspects

Aspects are the relationship of the planets to one another. They are the conversations or dialogue that happens when planets relate.

Conjunction: A conjunction is the most powerful aspect, and it takes place when two planets occupy the same or nearly the same degree of the zodiac. It represents a fusion of the two planets and their energies. The New Moon is actually a conjunction of the Sun and Moon.

Opposition: This is when two planets are directly opposite each other, separated by 180 degrees. It signifies polarization or tension.

This tension can add depth and character to the birth chart. A Full Moon is an opposition of the Sun and Moon.

Trine: This is when two planets are separated by 120 degrees. It signifies a harmonious and flowing relationship between the two planets. Considered a fortunate aspect, a trine isn't all it's cracked up to be, as trines can let us *coast* rather than achieve.

Sextile: Sixty degrees apart, a sextile is like a baby trine. It's a supportive aspect; both planets are energized by each other. It's easy to remember because it has the word "sex" in it.

Square: A square has a ninety-degree separation. When two planets square each other, there is friction. Like an opposition, a square has the reputation for being "negative," yet it often results in action and productivity.

The Elements: The four elements are fire, earth, air, and water. They describe the basic qualities or temperaments of the sign.

* *Fire signs* (Aries, Leo, and Sagittarius) represent courage, drive, energy, and self-assertion.

* *Earth signs* (Taurus, Virgo, and Capricorn) represent stability, practicality, patience, and reliability.

* *Air signs* (Gemini, Libra, and Aquarius) represent intelligence, communication, alertness, and social skills.

* *Water signs* (Cancer, Scorpio, and Pisces) represent emotion, sensitivity, depth, and subjectivity.

Some Things You May Like to Know

The planets don't cause things to happen. What they do is *expose* or *reveal* what's already going on. For instance, when Pluto (the planet of life, death, and transformation) entered the sign Capricorn (business, banking, corporations) in 2008, the economy crashed. Pluto didn't *cause* the crash, but it *exposed* what wasn't working in those systems.

The term "retrograde" is misleading. The planets don't actually move backward; they merely appear that way from here on Earth. Astrologically, this means that the energy of the retrograde planet is *reversed*. It's as if the planet were on sabbatical, and we can't depend on it in the normal way. It's not bad, for it allows us to rethink that planet's energies.

"Mercury retrograde" has a reputation for causing trouble, but you simply have to know how to use it. It's not a good time to buy Mercury-ruled items such as computers, cell phones, and cars. It also tends to coincide with delays and setbacks in travel, traffic, and communication. Although you wouldn't want to *begin* something important (like getting married or buying a house), it's excellent for taking care of *old business.* Think of the prefix re: *redo, revisit, rethink,* and *rewrite.* It's also a perfect time to purchase vintage clothes, find treasures at a yard sale, and buy used items on eBay. You might even run into people from your past.

Countries, cities, and states all have charts. What is known as *mundane astrology* studies society rather than individuals. For instance, America, born on July 4, 1776, has a compassionate Cancer Sun (we want to take care of the whole world) with a free-spirited Aquarius Moon (we were founded by rebels) and a feisty Sagittarius Rising (the symbol of the cowboy).

Corporations also have charts. There is a branch of astrology that specializes in business and finance. J. Pierpont Morgan, the wealthy American financier at the turn of the century who financed companies such United States Steel Corporation and the Northern Pacific Railway, used astrology for business. He said, "Anyone can be a millionaire, but to become a billionaire, you need an astrologer."

It's all good. There is no such thing as a bad chart or a bad aspect. Hopefully, we all have some great aspects in our birth chart, as well as some challenging ones. Why challenging ones? We're here to learn. The hard aspects are the ones that push us to grow, change, and achieve. Too many "easy" aspects can make us lazy. Nothing is written in stone. We all have free will. The chart represents potential. Ultimately, it is up to us what we do with it.

Astrology can be summed up in the timeless maxim: as above, so below. What is written in the heavens is encoded in us, and what is encoded in us is also in the heavens. It's another way of saying we are all connected, and the universe is inherently a meaningful place. The birth chart is a map of the heavens, a tool to understanding what is written both above and below, a guide to our journey toward becoming actualized.

THE CYCLES

THE SATURN RETURN
Growing Up and Getting Real (Age 29)

The lesson of Saturn is that life is a lesson.

Saturn is one of those planets with a terrible reputation and even worse PR. No wonder: It's associated with reality, responsibility, seriousness, setbacks, caution, fear, limitations, and obstacles. Oh, and let's not leave out old age! Ancient astrologers referred to Saturn as the Great Malefic; it's also known as the Lord of Winter, the Taskmaster of the Universe, and the Great Teacher.

I call Saturn the "Dr. Phil" of planets; it's about *getting real.* Saturn is a no frills kind of guy, but it isn't *bad;* no planet is. Let's compare Saturn to Jupiter—a planet with great PR and terrific buzz. Jupiter has a reputation for bestowing luck, prosperity, and abundance, yet this planet isn't all it's cracked up to be. Bigger-is-better Jupiter, like certain politicians and rock stars, also rules excess and exaggeration—it's where we can't say "no."

Bottom line: Jupiter isn't all good luck and Lotto, and Saturn isn't all struggle and sacrifice. It's said that Jupiter gives us crutches, while Saturn takes them away. At some point, we need to remove the training wheels or, like Forrest Gump, throw off the braces. The gift of Saturn is that it teaches us self-discipline, self-control, good boundaries, and, above all, maturity. Not exciting or sexy qualities but absolutely necessary if we want to create anything of lasting value.

Saturn's Backstory

Saturn comes by its reputation legitimately. The planet was named after the mythic Titan, known to the Greeks as Cronus and to the Romans as Saturn, who fathered gods but also devoured his children, just like his father before him. In fact, Saturn castrated his father (Uranus, also spelled Ouranus) with his sickle, which is how he became ruler of the Universe. Saturn married his sister Rhea; together they reigned for countless ages.

It had been prophesied that one of Saturn's children would depose him. To prevent this from happening he swallowed each of his progeny immediately after Rhea gave birth. Finally, after the birth of their sixth child (Zeus/Jupiter), Rhea had had enough. Rhea had baby Zeus secretly taken away to the island of Crete to be raised by nursemaids. Rhea then wrapped a stone in swaddling clothes and gave it to Saturn; he swallowed it, believing it was the infant.

When Zeus was grown, he returned, and, with the help of his grandmother (Gaia), he poisoned his father, causing Saturn to vomit up the other five children: Hestia, Demeter, Hera, Hades, and Poseidon. A devastating war between these new gods (the Olympians) and the older gods (the Titans) followed, almost destroying the entire universe. Ultimately, Zeus and the Olympians won, and

Saturn and his brothers (the other Titans) were imprisoned in Tartarus, a dark, forbidding region far below the earth.

Law and Order

In astrology, the planet Jupiter is associated with justice and the legal system. Saturn, on the other hand, represents those figures who *enforce* the law: the policeman, the drill sergeant, the principal, the mother superior, the CIA. Saturn is related to authority and our earliest encounters with it. Ultimately, Saturn teaches us to become the *author* of our own lives. Saturn rules structures, the external structures of society that keeps us safe (but can also confine us) as well as our skeletal system, spine, and the skin that contain us. Saturn also governs the knees, and encounters with this Great Teacher often "bring us to our knees."

> *He has none of the glamour associated with the outer planets*
> *and none of the humanness of the personal planets.*
> —Liz Greene (*Saturn: A New Look at an Old Devil*)

We all have the planet Saturn somewhere in our chart. We can't have it surgically removed (though some celebrities have tried—you know who I mean), and we can't hold back Father Time, another name for Saturn. The sign and house where we have Saturn is where we are cautious, slow, and often stuck; it's an area that doesn't come naturally or easily. As a result, we have to work on it, which is why we often become proficient in that area. It's the little girl who takes ice skating lessons to strengthen her weak ankles and becomes an Olympic champion or the kid who stutters and ends up being a famous actor or public speaker.

The good news is that Saturn gets better with age. More good news: unlike Jupiter, Saturn doesn't shower us with gifts, but it is fair and does reward us at the end of the transit. If we work with Saturn, we will be paid accordingly—but not a penny more! Another name for Saturn is the Lord of Karma; we reap what we sow.

The Saturn Return

Everything changes at our Saturn Return; I mean *everything*. This is the big Kahuna, the doorway to adulthood, and to the first major adult life cycle. Once a year, the Sun comes back, or *returns,* to the exact position it was in when we were born; that is our *Solar Return*—or what is commonly called our birthday. Saturn takes approximately twenty-nine and a half years to return to its birth position. Voilà, it is our Saturn birthday, or *Saturn Return*. People talk about the big 3-0; it's really the big 2-9.

Something happens in our mid- to late twenties: we begin to feel the clock ticking; there is a sneaking sensation that we're running out of time, and we need to make some important decisions—like where we're going and what we plan to do with our life. It doesn't matter how important your job is (running a major corporation, bestselling author, raising a family), how much money you're making, or how many Twitter followers and Facebook friends you have. There is a part of us that remains connected to our parents and their standards—or perhaps is still rebelling against them. That doesn't negate what we've accomplished during our twenties, but on some level we are operating within the context of the family we grew up in. At our Saturn Return, it's time to discover who *we* are, what *we* believe in, and make some decisions based on *our* values and interests.

Saturn doesn't ask us to give up our dreams, only to make them real.
—Steven Forrest

Maybe you dream of being a rock star. You're passionate about music; you've got some serious guitar skills and a decent voice; and the band you formed in high school was a local legend. You and your buddies move to New York City, and the band gets some gigs; just enough to keep your hopes up but not enough to really take off.

By your mid-twenties, you're getting tired of sharing an apartment in the boondocks of Brooklyn with three other guys and eating cold pizza for breakfast. Over the years, you've done temp work to make extra money. One day, you're sent to a recording studio and become fascinated; the work is stimulating and the people are great. The temp job evolves into a full-time position. You've finally found your niche.

Here's another scenario: the band dissolves, your girlfriend breaks up with you, and you hit bottom. After weeks of feeling sorry for yourself, you realize that it's now or never and decide to get serious about your music. You cut back on the late nights and drinking, write a half dozen new songs that finally have some real feeling, and make a demo. Maybe, like Adam Lambert (who, in 2009 at age twenty-seven, came in second on *American Idol*), you audition for a reality television singing competition and your career finally takes off. Whatever you decide to undertake will involve compromise, sacrifices, and bloody hard work. That's just how Saturn operates, but at our Return, we're finally ready, willing, and humble enough to do that.

Saturn is associated with our professional life and status, so for many of us, our Saturn Return involves a career decision. That can mean discovering what we want to do; or, if we're already working in a field we love, we might take on more responsibility, get a promotion, or go into business for ourselves. Some of us may already be working in demanding and highly skilled professions, even saving lives and contributing to society. In that case we may decide to commit to a relationship or start a family.

For example, Kate Middleton and Prince William were both born in 1982 and have Saturn in Libra (they take relationships seriously). They were married in 2011 during their Saturn Return.

Other people may decide to go back to school for an advanced degree, buy a home, or volunteer for a cause they are passionate about.

By the time she was twenty-nine, Celine Dion had achieved stardom; she had made twenty-five albums and was at the top of her career. She wanted desperately to have a child but couldn't get pregnant. Finally, in 1999, during her Saturn Return, she made a difficult decision; she put her career on hold to start a family as well as to help her husband recover from cancer. She gave birth to a son in 2001. When she returned to her career, critics noted that her music had a more mature sound.

Natalie Portman was already a major star when she signed on for the role of the young ballerina in the movie *Black Swan*. The preparation for the role was grueling; although she had studied dance when she was younger, Portman was required to train for five to six hours a day for six months. It paid off; Natalie Portman won the Academy Award for best actress for *Black Swan*. She also met her husband while working on the film, the choreographer Benjamin Millepied, and became pregnant.

It doesn't matter how much potential we have; sooner or later, we must prove ourselves to the world. Whether it's a career, a family, or a role in the world, we dedicate ourselves to something that will occupy a good part of our adult life and come to define us. We can't dream forever; there comes a time when we need to grow up, take a stand, and put our dreams to the test. The Saturn Return is that time. How do we know what that will be? Around the age of twenty-seven, something begins to happen that will give us a clue.

The Progressed Lunar Return

Progressions are another predictive technique that illustrates how we develop and evolve throughout life. The progressed lunar cycle (sometimes called the Moon cycle) moves almost at the same speed as the Saturn cycle, but it takes around twenty-seven, rather than twenty-nine, years to complete. The Moon is the domain of emotion and instinct; Saturn represents reality, form, and structure.

Before we figure out what we need to *do,* we get a feeling, an impulse. In other words, *being* comes before *doing;* inspiration comes before action. Imagine going to a Broadway musical or an opera. Before the curtain goes up and the action begins, there is the overture. We hear the music and immediately get a sense of the story. Is it *The Lion King, Les Miserables,* or *Hamilton?* The overture tells us what to expect.

The lunar cycle that precedes the Saturn Return is our overture. If we are quiet, pay attention, and listen to our intuition, we can *feel* something; an impulse that's beginning to grow, a tiny melody telling us what will happen when the curtain rises. Astrologer Steven Forrest has said: "If you haven't taken the time to feel at the Lunar Return, you end up making a random choice and have a random chance of being happy. The lunar has to be gotten right; it lays the foundation inwardly and invisibly."

Let yourself be silently drawn by the strange pull of what you really love.
—Rumi

First we dream: that happens at our lunar time; that is our *inner process.* We are pregnant with something; we are incubating who we will be as an adult, and it must be nurtured and protected. In the Saturn time, we bring that dream into manifestation; that is the *outer process.* It is then that the two come together. We are a society of multitaskers—overscheduled, overextended, and often overwhelmed. Our culture does not honor the lunar, the feminine. We don't receive a lot of support for slowing down, going inside, and listening to those subtle impulses. But that's exactly what we need to do during this lunar time—if the Saturn Return is going to be fulfilled.

The 27 Club: Road Under Construction. Slow Down. Danger Ahead

There are many examples of people who have departed either before, during, or right after their Saturn Return; so many, in fact, that there's a name for it: the 27 Club. Janis Joplin, Jimi Hendrix, Jim Morrison, and Brian Jones were all members. So was Kurt Cobain; in fact, according to his sister, he spoke about wanting to join the 27 Club, and he succeeded. Robert Downey Jr. *almost* became a member. Amy Winehouse was terrified that she would become a member and ultimately did.

The price of joining this exclusive club is high, but you can't put it on your Visa or Black Amex. Instead, it will cost you your life. The 27 Club, also known as the Forever Club, is reserved for those people—specifically famous rock musicians—who have died around the age of twenty-seven, often under mysterious circumstances. There are songs, a movie, books, and even websites devoted to it.

Many other musicians have died close to that age: Otis Redding (26), Hank Williams (29), and Jeff Buckley (29). In fact, Jeff Buckley was second generation; his father, musician Tim Buckley, died at twenty-eight. And it's not just musicians; there have also been poets (Rupert Brooke), artists (Jean-Michel Basquiat), and movie stars (Heath Ledger) who have joined this club. Why are the mid- to late twenties filled with so many landmines? Why are rock stars and creative people particularly vulnerable?

The Progressed Lunar Return is a time to slow down, to get in touch with our feelings, and to allow our intuition to guide us to the great task we will undertake at our Saturn Return. For most of us, this is doable. The problem arises if you're living on the fast track, running on empty, and self-medicating when you're twenty-six and twenty-seven. In that case, it's much harder to listen to your heart; and if you try, the information being filtered through a heavy haze of booze and drugs isn't likely to be reliable. In fact, following what you think is your heart could be extremely dangerous. Insecurities, fears, and doubts become exaggerated; so can the need to escape.

Many people get sober and clean up their act at their Saturn Return. Actors Bradley Cooper and Rob Lowe stopped drinking at age twenty-nine, and both have been very open about how it has changed their lives for the better. For those who have serious emotional or psychological issues, this period can be a slippery slope.

For the majority of us, the Saturn Return is a challenging but empowering period. By committing to something and following through, we learn discipline, decision making, and how to function in the world. But what if you achieved massive fame and fortune in your teens or early twenties, before you acquired those Saturn skills? What if you have access to endless drugs, sex, and fast cars, plus a team of lawyers to bail you out when trouble hits? It takes an exceptional young person with high self-esteem, good values, and a strong family not to yield to temptation. Many members of the 27 Club came from broken families with histories of alcohol or drug abuse. Once they became famous, they had handlers and hangers-on instead of positive role models.

The Moon is emotional; it *feels*. At the lunar time, we must tune into our Moon, our mood. Can you sense what it's asking of you? Can you hear the call, and can you respond? Saturn is practical; it wants to build something real and tangible. It asks us to take what's inside us (a dream, a vision, a goal) and manifest it in the world in a concrete way. Saturn won't do the work for us; it is up to us to take responsibility for our vision, do the heavy lifting, and see it through to the end. Bottom line: You find your mountain and then you climb it.

Saturn thrives on massive amounts of hard work. In fact, Saturn has never seen a job it didn't like.

What to Expect

Like any initiation, the Saturn Return isn't easy—if it's easy, it ain't Saturn. This is not about instant gratification; this is about long-term goals and dedication. Most likely, there will be challenges, obstacles, and setbacks. The workload can be tremendous, the road long, problems and pressures daunting. That's all part of the process.

Randy Pausch (the Carnegie Mellon professor of computer science who became famous for his inspiring book, *The Last Lecture*) inadvertently described Saturn perfectly when he said, "The brick walls are there for a reason. The brick walls are not there to keep us out. The brick walls are there to give us a chance to show how badly we want something."

The Saturn Return Brings a Mentor

Often during an initiation, a mentor or guide will appear to help us make the transition. When it's our Saturn Return, the mentor is generally older, although not necessarily in age; he or she may be someone with more experience, wisdom, or gravitas.

It was shortly after his Saturn Return that Carl Jung initiated contact with Freud; they met the following year. Although Jung's reputation in Zurich was growing, he spent the next several years apprenticed to Freud. In 1928, when Georgia O'Keeffe was twenty-nine, Alfred Stieglitz included her in a group show at his gallery in New York City. It was a small show, but it was a turning point; Stieglitz not only helped launch O'Keeffe's career, he became her lover and later her husband. Johnny Carson was a mentor to both Joan Rivers and Jerry Seinfeld. They both appeared on his show at their Saturn Return.

We May Move to the Place Where Our Work Will Begin

At her Saturn Return, Karen von Blixen-Finecke (better known by her pen name, Isak Dinesen) left Denmark for Kenya, where she and her husband established their coffee plantation. Gertrude Stein moved to Paris, where she launched her famous salon. In 1948, when he was twenty-nine, J. D. Salinger submitted a story to the *New Yorker* entitled "A Perfect Day for Bananafish." The magazine was so impressed that they signed him to a contract; Salinger found his literary home. In 1983, Oprah Winfrey, then twenty-nine, relocated to Chicago to host WLS-TV's *A.M. Chicago*. Within months, her show overtook that of Phil Donahue and became the highest-rated daytime talk show.

It Can Be a Humbling Experience

In many ways, the Saturn Return can be compared to going into the army, rehab, or one of those wilderness experiences such as Outward Bound. Our addictions, our freedom, even our identity are taken away, and we're forced to shape up. There's usually a Saturn figure (like a sergeant, Alcoholics Anonymous [AA] sponsor, or team captain) involved. Let's face it: in our twenties we are untried and untested, yet often arrogant and full of ourselves; we need direction. It's a dirty job, but someone has to do it. The beauty of Saturn is that, at their best, experiences like the army or rehab force us to grow up; they teach us discipline, responsibility, and accountability. It can be harsh, even brutal, but we are forever changed.

Jack Kerouac completed *On the Road* in 1951 when he was twenty-nine; it took him until 1957 to find a publisher (Viking Press). Poet Mary Oliver published her first book of poems, *No Voyage and Other Poems*, in 1963 when she was twenty-eight. Hillary and Bill got married at their Saturn Returns (she was twenty-eight; he was twenty-nine). Both Bill Clinton and Al Gore entered politics during their Saturn Returns, while Hillary Clinton joined the Rose law firm. Patti Smith released her first album, *Horses*. Diane von Fürstenberg started her fashion company when she was twenty-three, but it was at her Saturn Return that she introduced her famous knitted "jersey wrap" dress that would shoot her to success. Harrison Ford, Sylvester Stallone, and Meryl Streep all got their big break at their Saturn Return.

Musicians and bands typically burst on the scene during their early years, but the Saturn Return can bring other changes. The Beatles had their biggest hits during 1965–1969. They broke up in 1970; John Lennon and Ringo Starr were both thirty, Paul McCartney was twenty-eight, and George Harrison was twenty-seven.

Carole King, along with her husband Gerry Goffin, wrote dozens of hits for other artists. In 1971 (at age twenty-nine), King released her breakthrough album *Tapestry*, one of the bestselling albums of all time. At age thirty, saxophonist Clarence Clemons joined Bruce Springsteen's E Street Band. In 1974, at age twenty-nine, the Wailers broke up, and Bob Marley went on to pursue a solo career.

Do you remember the 2009 film, *Julie & Julia*? The movie is based on the true story of Julie Powell. Julie, then twenty-nine, was working at an office job in Manhattan—and she hated it. One day, she met her old college roommates for lunch; all had high-powered jobs, and one woman was a successful blogger. When Julie told her boyfriend about the lunch and how dissatisfied she was with her own career, he suggested that she try blogging. "What could I blog about?" she asked. The boyfriend suggested that, since she loved to cook, she should blog about that. Julie decided to cook every recipe in Julia Child's book, *Mastering the Art of French Cooking*, in one year. Every night after coming home from the office, Julie spent hours boiling lobsters or deboning ducks, then stayed up late writing her blog. She wasn't looking for fame and fortune; Julie had no idea her blog would lead to a book deal or that Nora Ephron would someday direct Meryl Streep in the film adaption of the book. Julie was hungry (pun intended) for a challenge and for work she was passionate about.

What It Looks Like When We Fail

There is no shame in not having your life together at twenty-eight or twenty-nine when Saturn kicks in. Many of us are late bloomers. We're not talking about perfection; it's about beginning the process, taking on responsibility, and dedicating ourselves to something we believe in. When that doesn't happen, we end up being stuck in an old persona or situation that no longer fits.

When that happens, it's easy to become bitter, cynical, and self-righteous. Blaming others is not unusual. It's always "them"—our parents, the government, the economy, or just plain bad luck. Or we go to the other extreme and end up blaming ourselves. We continue to drift, sell out, or take the easy road; marry for the wrong reason or find work that is dull. Saturn is associated with depression, and, although not a prediction, it is one of the ways Saturn can express itself when it doesn't have a healthy outlet.

> **Saturn Wisdom:** Thomas Mann said in his novel, *Joseph and His Brothers,* "At thirty, a man steps out of the darkness and wasteland of preparation into active life; it is the time to show oneself, the time of fulfillment."

People with Saturn Prominent in Their Chart

Carl Jung, Jimmy Carter, and Bono all have Saturn in the first house, an extremely solid placement that indicates a powerful work ethic and drive. Lin-Manuel Miranda has both his Sun and Moon in Capricorn, the sign that Saturn rules. Alexander Hamilton, who inspired Lin-Manuel's award winning Broadway show, was also born with his Sun and Moon in Capricorn. It's not unusual for actors who portray a historical figure or authors who write about them to have compatible charts.

> *Just begin.*
> —John Cage

The Saturn Return is especially important because it is the first major life cycle. We cross over from youth into adulthood, and, in doing so, we're laying the foundation for all the other cycles and for the rest of our life. No pressure. We don't have to have everything figured out or know all the answers. Our projects may not involve record deals, the red carpet, or the cover of *Rolling Stone*. Beginnings are often subtle, quiet, and deceptively inauspicious. This cycle can start modestly: we take a few classes at a community college; we apprentice in a bakery; we get sober and join AA; we commit to a relationship. And although we're focused on creating something in the outer world, the Saturn Return is also an inner process; the skills we develop and the relationships we form during this time are helping us to build character.

Mensch is a Yiddish word that literally means "a good person," but it goes deeper than that. To say someone is a mensch is a great compliment. It has to do with character; a mensch is a decent, noble person, a stand-up guy. He (or she) is the kind of person who strives to always do the right thing, rather than the easy thing. In many ways, the Saturn Return teaches us the necessary skills we need to become a mensch.

What's the Timing of Your Saturn Return, or How Long Will Saturn Be Messing with You?

Saturn is in a sign for about two and a half years. That doesn't mean you are under pressure all that time. Transiting Saturn generally connects with your birth Saturn two or three times during that period. In a way, you're in Saturn School; when it makes an exact aspect (to your birth Saturn), the final exams take place. The stakes are higher; you push harder, but that's when you receive the rewards.

The Saturn Square:
Saturn at Age Thirty-six—Growing Pains

The middle of the thirties is literally the midpoint of life. The halfway mark. No gong rings, of course. But twinges begin.
—Gail Sheehy, *Passages: Predictable Crises of Adult Life*

A little over seven years after its return, Saturn makes an opening square to its natal position. It's like getting our report card: Here's me; here's my life. How am I doing? The Saturn Return at twenty-nine is a conjunction and the most powerful aspect; it signals a beginning, and beginnings have energy, promise, and potential— even those orchestrated by Saturn.

Maybe we decide to start our own company, get pregnant, or quit our corporate job and retreat to a cabin in Maine to write our novel. Just the act of making the decision and taking a stand for something can be energizing. It is the hero starting off on her journey, and, although we may not know the road ahead or how it will turn out, there's a sense of adventure and anticipation. However, at the square, we have to deal with the results of our decision. In a sense, the honeymoon is over.

Seven is a special number; it appears everywhere—from references in occult and religious traditions to the seven days of the week, seven notes in a musical scale, and seven colors of the rainbow. The great teacher Rudolph Steiner taught extensively about the seven-year cycles that continue throughout our life. Edgar Cayce's psychic readings are filled with references to them. The term "seven-year itch" refers to the tension that often occurs in a relationship, causing partners to either divorce or adapt. Which brings us to Saturn. Every seven years, Saturn makes an aspect to its natal position; it takes us back to reality, and we are invited to reevaluate what we are doing in the external world.

In her book *Passages,* Gail Sheehy gives the example of a crustacean, who, in order to grow, must shed a series of protective shells. She writes: "With each passage some magic must be given up, some cherished illusion of safety and comfortably familiar sense of self must be cast off, to allow for the greater expansion of our own distinctiveness."

At the Saturn square, there can be success, financial security, maybe even fame. Yet success can bring a whole new set of problems to negotiate. Having a child is a miracle, but it's also demanding. Starting our own company brings more responsibility and less freedom. We may finish our novel and even get it published, but we may be at a loss as to what to write next. There are consequences to be dealt with, adjustments to be made, fine tuning.

No matter what the original vision was, this is often a time to go back to the drawing board. The future may appear less rosy but it's *real.* The Saturn square at age thirty-six comes right before midlife, which is the next big cycle. It's a period when we naturally begin to question our life and our decisions. Gail Sheehy called this the "Deadline Decade."

At age twenty-nine, Gloria Steinem wrote her now famous article for *Show* magazine about the New York Playboy Club. Entitled "A Bunny's Tale," the article would change her life. At the time, she was not yet a feminist; it was 1963, and the movement was just beginning. But a seed had been planted, and she began to look at things differently. By 1970, the time Saturn made its opening square, she had fully embraced feminism and was recognized as a leader. That same year, *Newsweek* magazine put Gloria Steinem on the cover. In 1971, *Ms.* magazine was born, cofounded by Gloria.

But this exposure came at a price. Steinem was criticized by conservatives as well as by the senior women in the feminist movement. The media often reported on her looks and not her message. Steinem's growing fame put her in front of large audiences, which terrified her. Many times she cancelled speaking engagements at the last minute, which resulted in her being blacklisted from some events. Nevertheless, she persevered and found a way to make it work. She joined other women, such as civil rights lawyer Florynce Kennedy, and they spoke to audiences as a team. "Nervousness might still return, like malaria, but mostly I'd learned that audiences turn into partners if you just listen to them as much as you talk," she wrote in *My Life on the Road*.

Coinciding with the Saturn square, the Jupiter Return takes place at age thirty-six, bringing fresh energy and optimism. This often concurs with a promotion, raise, or an opportunity to broaden our horizons. Jupiter rules education, higher learning, religion, and long-distance travel. This period can bring opportunities to expand our circle of friends and mentors, who can influence our thinking, values, and ultimately our direction in life. This was certainly true for Gloria Steinem and the many people in politics and the women's movement that she met during this time in her life.

Every twelve years we get a Jupiter Return; Jupiter comes back to the position it occupied at birth at ages twelve, twenty-four, thirty-six, and so on. Jupiter is the largest planet apart from the Sun. In Roman mythology, Jupiter (the Greek Zeus) was king of the gods, and he threw lavish parties and bestowed gifts on the other gods and mortals. Jupiter can shower us with blessings and lucky breaks, but the secret is to get Jupiter's attention by taking action and extending yourself into new territory. Jupiter is about faith. How much faith do you have in yourself to go for something you want? Be audacious, take some risks—that's when the magic kicks in!

At our Jupiter Return, we are also planting a seed, setting something in motion that will unfold over the following twelve years; make it conscious.

Bill Clinton accomplished a lot during his Saturn Return. Shortly after he married Hillary in October 1975, he announced that he was running for attorney general in Arkansas. He won the election easily, and in 1978, at age thirty-two, he went on to become the youngest governor in the country. He also became the youngest ex-governor. Although he focused on educational reform and improving Arkansas's roads, he was criticized for an unpopular motor vehicle tax and for his handling of the Cuban refugees detained at Fort Chafee. As a result, he lost the reelection in 1980.

Being a Leo, he may have had some of the lion's legendary hubris. It's not unusual for Leos to experience a failure early in their career so as to learn humility. Forced to start over, Clinton apologized for his errors, asked voters to give him another chance, and, by the time Saturn made a square to its natal position, he was elected governor again. He remained in office for ten years, during which he increased Arkansas's economy and transformed the educational system from the worst in the nation to one of the best.

Lin-Manuel Miranda read Ron Chernow's biography of Alexander Hamilton while on vacation in 2007. He was twenty-seven years old and experiencing his Progressed Lunar Return. He was so inspired by the book that he wrote a rap about Hamilton for the

White House Evening of Poetry, Music, and Spoken Word, which took place in 2009. At that time, he was having his Saturn Return. By 2012, Miranda was performing a collection of the songs based on the life of Hamilton and referred to as the *Hamilton Mixtape*. This musical (now just *Hamilton*) officially opened on Broadway on August 6, 2015, to rave reviews. He was thirty-five years old. Miranda is an excellent example of inspiration (Lunar Return), manifestation (Saturn), and mastery (the Saturn square).

Daring Greatly

The willingness to show up changes us. It makes us a little braver each time.
—Brené Brown, *Daring Greatly: How the Courage to Be Vulnerable Transforms the Way We Live, Love, Parent, and Lead*

I'm a big fan of Brené Brown and her books *Daring Greatly* and *Rising Strong*. For me, *Daring Greatly* is a great metaphor for our Saturn Return. The title comes from Theodore Roosevelt's speech "Citizen of a Republic," sometimes referred to simply as "The Man in the Arena." It's about our willingness to step into the arena, engage with our vulnerability, and be seen. In *Rising Strong: The Reckoning. The Rumble. The Revolution,* Brown deals with what happens when we fall. Because, let's face it, if we put ourselves out there, at some point we will stumble; we may fail. For me, *Rising Strong* represents the Saturn square at thirty-six. It's about examining our choices, making the necessary corrections, and having the courage to continue.

My Saturn Return

To say that I was drifting during my twenties is an understatement. In the early 1960s, I was nineteen, restless, and confused; so I decided to go to Europe with a one-way ticket and a few hundred dollars. I had begun modeling in high school, but the stress at home plus my eating disorder derailed that dream. I moved to New York and did some acting, but mostly I worked as a dancer in clubs like the Copacabana and the Peppermint Lounge. With that somewhat checkered résumé, I headed to Rome. There was plenty of acting work in American coproductions, as well as in Italian films. And—because the Italians dubbed everything—you didn't even have to speak the language! It was like the Wild West—anything was possible.

I was able to find work immediately in films such as *Gidget Goes to Rome, The Pink Panther,* and *The Agony and the Ecstasy.* No major roles, but it was enough to get by. Life in Rome was cheap, colorful, and laid back. Many of the films were shot on location, so I was able to work in places like Belgrade, Budapest, and Greece. I traveled, went to film festivals, met amazing people, and had lots of exciting adventures, but I still didn't have a clue as to what I really wanted. I was passionate about films, but I hated the *business* of show business. I simply didn't know what else to do. I was young and photogenic. Everyone told me I should be in films, so I went along with it.

After several years, I grew disillusioned with both Rome and acting. I became severely depressed. It was then that I decided to move back to New York City and get into therapy. A producer I knew asked me to collaborate on a screenplay; although the screenplay was never produced, it led to a job as a story editor and screenwriter with a major film company. On the surface, my life may have looked enviable (more film festivals, more travel), but it didn't feel like *my* life. Truth be told, the job, like everything else I had done up until then, was connected to a man. Could I do something on my own and, if so, what? I was determined to find out. I was passionate about food, so I decided to open a restaurant.

It was the early seventies; the health food craze was gaining momentum, but the food itself was bland and boring, consisting mainly of items like carrot loafs, brown rice, and homemade breads that could sink a ship. I had a vision of healthful food that was also delicious and sensual. I wanted to combine natural ingredients with gourmet recipes. And that's exactly what I did.

In 1974, I opened a natural food restaurant on 10th Street in Greenwich Village called Whole Wheat 'n Wild Berrys. I had never attended culinary school or apprenticed with a chef or even *worked* in a restaurant, apart from the occasional waitressing job while I was pursuing acting. I had *no* experience—not something I would recommend, by the way. I had yet another handicap; since my teens, I had suffered from a crippling eating disorder. My life revolved around eating and dieting—the reason I first became interested in health foods. Plus, in 1974, the stock market had plunged—everybody told me it was the worst possible time to go into business. But I sensed it was *my time,* and I needed to do something.

I didn't realize that I had something on my side: Saturn. I was ready to take on a big challenge; I was even prepared to face my dysfunctional relationship with food and get the monkey—or in this case the muffin—off my back. I remember thinking, "Either I'll end up weighing three hundred pounds, or I'll beat this."

The world was ready for my vision of natural food, and I was ready to work hard. I loved going to the restaurant every day, coming up with new recipes, working with the staff, connecting with customers. I actually welcomed the long hours and double shifts! Friends wondered why I would give up my life of film festivals and traveling abroad to deal with the craziness of the restaurant business, but I was happy to finally have something to call my own.

I'm not going to lie and say it was always easy—it wasn't. I knew a little about health foods and cooking but nothing about preparing food on a large scale—and even less about the logistics of setting up and running a business. There wasn't a day or an hour when I wasn't having to deal with broken equipment, an unhappy chef, a problem with the food, or a flood in the basement. The most challenging thing of all was that every single day I had to face my worst fears: peanut butter pie, warm scones, moist gingerbread with homemade whipped cream, and lush cheesecake! But I hung in, I learned, I hired better and better people, and I worked really hard. The restaurant became a success, and I thrived. I eventually even healed my eating disorder. Saturn was a superb teacher.

Everyone has a Saturn Return; whether you're an A-list celebrity with an entourage, the president of a country, a waitress, a single parent, or a homeless person. Saturn doesn't exclude *anyone,* and it doesn't play favorites; it demands the same level of accountability and dedication from each and every one of us.

* You find something you want to do, make a commitment, and work hard to see it through.

* You don't complain or whine; you don't cheat or back down.

The rewards of the Saturn Return aren't necessarily flashy, but they are solid. You may not get gift bags and free passes, but ideally you'll receive something more important: self-worth, self-confidence, dignity, maturity, and a way to function in the world.

Hope begins in the dark, the stubborn hope that if you just show up and try to do the right thing, the dawn will come. You wait and watch and work: you don't give up.
—Anne Lamott

How to find out where your Saturn is: Thanks to the Internet, it's simple to get a free copy of your birth chart. Simply Google "free astrology chart" and type in your birth information (date, time, and location). Astrodienst, Café Astrology, and Astrolabe are three popular sites. Or just Google, "What sign was Saturn in during [the year you were born]."

Astrologer Steven Forrest (*www.forrestastrology.com*) offers a selection of excellent computerized astrology reports—both natal chart analysis and transits reports (what's currently happening)—at reasonable prices.

Get to Know Your Saturn

Where we have Saturn is where we have a buried treasure, but it takes tremendous work and effort to unearth it. Saturn is the karmic classroom, the playing field on which we are tested and pushed to our limits. Where we have Saturn is an area that is not fully developed, but if we work hard we can excel. Did you ever fail algebra or French and have to repeat it, maybe more than once? Remember the satisfaction when you *finally* got it? You *mastered* something.

If you have enough experiences like that, you start to feel pretty good about yourself. After a while, you gain confidence; you're able to aim higher and go farther. As Stephen Arroyo wrote in his book *Astrology, Karma, and Transformation,* "A remarkable inner strength can develop from Saturn's pressure, a strength that comes in part from knowing that we have done the required work, earned the results, and taken full responsibility for our own development."

Saturn is an important planet and a valuable ally. Get to know your own Saturn.

Saturn in Aries

Growing up, those with this Saturn may have been reprimanded for showing off. They want to shine, to feel like a star; often they do, once they find the right vehicle.

> **Their Greatest Fear:** They want desperately to be the center of attention but are terrified people won't like them.

> **They Need to Learn:** To trust their natural instincts, have fun, and not take themselves so seriously. They are here to learn independence, confidence, and especially patience.

> **Gifts:** Combine Aries's pioneering spirit with Saturn's discipline, and you get someone who can bring fresh ideas and bold originality to their chosen field.

> **Examples:** Albert Einstein, Florence Nightingale, Tina Turner, Celine Dion, Jennifer Aniston, Malala Yousafzai

Saturn in Taurus

These people may have been poor in childhood, or they grew up wealthy but were raised by nannies and ignored by their parents. They possess a powerful need for financial and emotional security.

> **Their Greatest Fear:** They will lose their home, their money, their position, and end up on the street. These people often have self-esteem issues.

> **They Need to Learn:** Not to place so much importance on material things and to love themselves for who they are and not what they own.

Gifts: Those with this Saturn placement are generous, trustworthy, dependable, and have great endurance. They are savvy about finances and real estate. They love beautiful things and have exquisite taste.

Examples: Pablo Picasso, Mother Teresa, Tina Fey, Bob Dylan, Martha Stewart, Muhammad Ali

Saturn in Gemini

Growing up, these people may not have been allowed to express themselves, and they kept their fears bottled up. They may have had difficulty with early education or have a slight learning disability. Often they have a high IQ—their minds just work differently.

Their Greatest Fear: They are afraid of being thought stupid and are self-conscious about their education.

They Need to Learn: They have difficulty confiding in others, but that's precisely what they need to do. Expressing themselves creatively through words or music also helps.

Gifts: Saturn adds discipline and steadiness to the Gemini's natural intelligence giving these people a capacity for thinking, writing, and problem solving. They are extremely curious, engaging conversationalists, and life-long students.

Examples: Sigmund Freud, Coco Chanel, Billie Holiday, Gwyneth Paltrow, Mick Jagger, Paul McCartney

Saturn in Cancer

Those with their Saturn in Cancer may have been disappointed or neglected by a parent and as a result seek approval from others. Should they fail to get it, they may build a wall around themselves.

> **Their Greatest Fear:** That they will be homeless or that they don't deserve a nice place to live. Owning a home and land helps. These people have trouble expressing their emotions for fear that they won't be accepted.

> **They Need to Learn:** To be self-sufficient rather than depend on others.

> **Gifts:** Once they heal their own issues, people with this Saturn placement make wonderful parents. They take family very seriously. Deeply caring, they make excellent counselors and loyal friends.

> **Examples:** Napoleon, Frank Sinatra, Ella Fitzgerald, Cher, George W. Bush, Angelina Jolie

Saturn in Leo

Those with this placement of Saturn are extremely talented but shy and have a love/hate relationship with the public. They can't go for the glamour; their work must serve a larger purpose.

> **Their Greatest Fear:** Those with Saturn in Leo crave attention and applause but are afraid of the spotlight. They worry that their gift won't be recognized or that it will be criticized.

They Need to Learn: Not to worry about what others think but to look within for the acknowledgment that they crave. They have massive creative blocks but must take their creativity seriously, believe in themselves, and never give up.

Gifts: These people are gifted artists as well, as being brilliant in business and politics. They have a genuine commitment to education.

Examples: Charlie Chaplin, Nelson Mandela, Hillary Clinton, Steven Spielberg, David Bowie, Kanye West

Saturn in Virgo

Health and work are their two obsessions. Those with Saturn in Virgo may have grown up around illness; either they are hypochondriacs, or they ignore their bodies. A parent may have had problems holding down a job.

Their Greatest Fear: Being out of work, which is why they often refuse to take a vacation. They fear chaos and often try to control things.

They Need to Learn: These people need to create balance in their lives and to know that they won't be punished if they have some fun. In fact, having fun is absolutely necessary for them.

Gifts: Skilled craftspeople and artists, no one works harder on themselves. These people care deeply for animals and the environment. They possess a strong sense of justice and integrity.

Examples: Bach, Prince Charles, Bruce Springsteen, Pope John Paul II, Richard Gere, Meryl Streep

Saturn in Libra

Libra is the ancient sign of marriage, so this group takes relationships seriously. They often marry young but have a better chance of having a happy union if they wait until they reach their Saturn Return.

> **Their Greatest Fear:** These people are aware that they can disappear in a relationship and are terrified of merging.

> **They Need to Learn:** To develop good boundaries and how to cooperate without giving away too much of themselves. Forgiveness is an important lesson.

> **Gifts:** Since Saturn rules the law, those with this placement make superb lawyers, judges, mediators, and negotiators. More than any other sign, they are willing to work on their relationships issues.

> **Examples:** Maria Callas, Tony Blair, Britney Spears, Roger Federer, Sting, Beyoncé

Saturn in Scorpio

Many of these people experienced emotional betrayal in childhood or lost a parent through death, divorce, or even simple neglect. This can leave them with scars but also bestows depth and understanding.

> **Their Greatest Fears:** These people crave intimacy but are terrified of their own passion and are afraid to surrender. They fear being financially dependent on anyone.

They Need to Learn: Not to be afraid of their hungers. They need to stop trying to control the world and just live in it.

Gifts: They seem to have some secret ability to rise up from humble beginnings and create great wealth and power. They are true survivors and can succeed at anything they put their minds to.

Examples: Carolos Castaneda, Marilyn Monroe, Amy Winehouse, Steve Jobs, Bill Gates, Oprah Winfrey

Saturn in Sagittarius

These people are serious in their pursuit of religion, philosophy, and higher education. They often develop a moral code or philosophy and can become very attached to it.

Their Greatest Fear: Sagittarians, the sign of the gypsy, are terrified of losing their freedom. Their reputation is important to them, and they fear being censored or ridiculed.

They Need to Learn: Patience, patience, and more patience. They need to become less judgmental and lose their "my way or the highway" attitude.

Gifts: They have high ethics and a love of honesty. They have the ability to turn their vision into a reality, inspire people, and attract followers.

Examples: Mahatma Gandhi, Martin Luther King Jr., Jackie Kennedy, Winston Churchill, Michael Jackson, Madonna

Saturn in Capricorn

This group is unswerving in its desire to succeed; since Saturn is strong in its own sign, they often do. Those among them who are unevolved can be ruthless.

Their Greatest Fear: They're afraid of their hunger for power. They fear authority, so they often become the authority.

They Need to Learn: It's not just about worldly success; they need to find a mission that is worthy of who they are. Becoming less rigid in their attitudes and having a sense of humor helps immensely.

Gifts: They are excellent organizers, extremely hard working, and disciplined. If they work on their issues and proceed with integrity, they can achieve tremendous success.

Examples: Marie Antoinette, Walt Disney, Princess Diana, Bono, Clint Eastwood, Taylor Swift

Saturn in Aquarius

Saturn can work well in this sign. Their minds are impersonal and scientific; the enlightened ones seek truth and have a strong sense of justice. These people want both freedom *and* stability.

Their Greatest Fear: They long to be like everyone else and desperately try to fit in.

They Need to Learn: To stop trying to conform; they are unique, which is perfectly okay. They need to learn that emotions are not a sign of weakness.

Gifts: They are dedicated to making this world a better place; if they find the right group or cause, they can create tremendous change. Friendship is their true religion; they're extremely loyal.

Examples: Mozart, Carl Jung, Gloria Steinem, Michelle Obama, Jim Carrey, Brad Pitt

Saturn in Pisces

Many with this placement of Saturn grew up in an environment that wasn't safe or rational. As a result, the world often feels unstable; they're easily overwhelmed, which makes them want to escape.

Their Greatest Fear: Fear itself. They are terrified of looking inside and confronting their own darkness, yet that's exactly what they need to do.

They Need to Learn: To find positive escapes (rather than negative ones). To know their vulnerability is their greatest gift. They need solitude and meditation to connect with their inner life.

Gifts: Their sensitivity makes them deeply compassionate; they have the capacity to be great healers, counselors, and artists. They have brilliant imaginations; they are the dreamers and visionaries who inspire the rest of us.

Examples: Sir Isaac Newton, Elisabeth Kübler-Ross, Kurt Cobain, Robert Redford, the Dalai Lama, Woody Allen

Stories
Helene's Story

There's a Pain Quotidian café in my neighborhood where I often go to write. It has a large upstairs area that is light and airy and quiet in the late afternoon. I recently got to talking to the manager, Helene. She told she was from Belgium, where she practiced law for five years.

Helene decided that she wanted to work more directly with people and took a job at Pain Quotidian (it's a Belgian company), where she trained to be a manager. They gave her a chance to move to New York to manage one of their locations.

I couldn't resist asking her age. Sure enough, she was twenty-eight. She knew all about the Saturn Return. "Friends told me it's the best age to make a career change."

Petra's Story

I think Sagittarians emerge from the womb with a passport clutched in their tiny little hands. That was certainly true of Petra. After graduating from Cornell with a degree in fine arts, she took off to see the world. She lived in Japan (where she modeled), France (where she has a grant to do art), and Italy.

Back in New York City, she drifted—she did some modeling and worked as a hostess at a trendy SoHo restaurant, but she didn't have any real focus. I remember telling her that it would come together at her Saturn Return. I probably sounded like a broken record.

Petra is one of the most creative people I know; she has a quirky but absolutely charming sense of style. It's not unusual for her to *make* a dress if she needs something to wear. For a while, Petra designed hats, and actually got them into Lord & Taylor, but she didn't have the financing to continue producing them. Finally, when her Saturn Return came around, she decided to study fashion at FIT (Fashion Institute of Technology). Bingo! It was as if, up to then, she had all the right ingredients but didn't have the recipe. Saturn is the recipe, the formula.

Petra graduated, did an internship in London with knitwear designer Julian McDonald, then found success designing knitwear for Saks Fifth Avenue, DKNY, and Oscar de la Renta.

Hannah's Story

My niece Hannah always wanted to be a nurse, and with her ambitious Capricorn Moon, she began early. By the time of her Saturn Return, she was running an emergency room in a hospital in Denver. She decided to go back to school to get her BSN (Bachelor of Science in Nursing), while working full time and making a long commute; a task worthy of Saturn in Virgo in the 6th house.

Jeremy's Story

Jeremy Geffen didn't even begin medical school until his Saturn Return. During his early twenties, he lived at an ashram in Florida. By the time he was twenty-five, he'd decided he wanted to study medicine.

He came to New York and enrolled in Columbia to do his premed; that is when I met him. Jeremy graduated from NYU medical school with honors and went on to become a board-certified oncologist and a pioneer in the field of integrative medicine. His book, *The Journey through Cancer: Healing and Transforming the Whole Person,* is one of the best on the subject.

THE MIDLIFE JOURNEY
Breakdowns and Breakthroughs (Ages 37–45)

In the middle of the journey of our life
I found myself within a dark woods
Where the straight way was lost.
—Dante Alighieri

It may start from the inside: a deep rumbling that seems to say, "Is that all there is?" Or it may come from the outside in the form of a crisis, such as a health challenge, a death in the family, or the loss of a job or a relationship. Either way, we end up feeling as if a hurricane has blasted through our lives and torn it wide open.

Although it may feel "sudden" and "appear" to come from the outside, if we're honest, we'll realize it's been brewing for a while; at some level, we've become stale and are playing small. Suddenly faced with our own mortality, we are forced to examine who we are and what we want. One thing is for sure: life as we know it will not remain the same, and if we handle it correctly, neither will we.

Whether we call "it" a midlife crisis, an identity crisis, or a deadline decade, this is life's most dramatic turning point. It ushers in the second major life cycle.

> *Somewhere between 35 and 45 if we let ourselves,*
> *most of us will have a full-out authenticity crisis.*
> —Gail Sheehy, *Passages*

Midlife is a complex period orchestrated by several planets and spread over a ten-year period from our mid-thirties to mid-forties. The sheer length of time it takes is what makes this period such a game-changer. Unlike the Saturn Return (which isn't exactly a day at the beach), during midlife, Pluto, Uranus, Neptune, *and* Saturn are all involved, and there isn't a lightweight amongst these planets. The good news (yes, there's good news) is that this is probably the greatest opportunity to break out of our old conditioning and liberate our finest potential. You see, midlife isn't just an event, it's a journey; like any great voyage, it's also an inner process, certain to change us if we pay attention.

> *A trip becomes "a journey" when you have lost your luggage.*
> —author unknown

So many great stories share a common theme. The heroine (or the hero) is suddenly thrown out of her familiar, comfortable life and thrust into foreign territory, often with nothing but the clothes on her back. She meets strange and extraordinary characters; some befriend her, others pose real danger, and all of them play an essential part in the story. Along the way, she is given tests that challenge her and adventures that empower her, until eventually she comes back to where she began. Everything is the same, but it is also different, because she has been transformed.

This theme is found in Dorothy's story in *The Wizard of Oz* and also in Homer's *Odyssey,* legends such as *Parsifal and the Holy Grail,* or the myth of Pluto's abduction of Persephone. We find it in *Dante's Divine Comedy, Star Wars, Avatar, Harry Potter,* and Elizabeth Gilbert's memoir, *Eat, Pray, Love.*

This tale is the Hero's Journey, and, when told well, it never fails to excite and inspire. It is indeed *our* story: the eternal journey of coming home to ourselves. As Glinda, the good witch, tells Dorothy at the end of the film, "You've always had the power, my dear; you just had to learn it for yourself." Yet to awaken that power, we must have the courage to leave what we know and enter the unknown, where nothing is certain, but everything is possible. *That* is the midlife process, and, just like the Hero's Journey, there are several phases.

Pluto

I would rather be whole than good.
—Carl Jung

The first stage of midlife is governed by Pluto, the planet of birth, death, and transformation. When we are around the age of thirty-six or thirty-seven, Pluto makes a square (a quarter turn) to its natal (birth) position. It is now time to face whatever we haven't resolved: our core issues, our worst fears, our deepest wound.

It's not unusual to experience a failure, loss, or betrayal that brings us to our knees; or perhaps there is no event, just the slow dawning that the life we're living is not the one we want. Pluto's job is to bring to the surface whatever we have repressed and ignored— all those broken and abandoned parts of ourselves that are buried in our unconscious. We can't change something unless we're aware of it. Pluto makes us aware.

The period in history that coincides with when a planet is discovered tells us a great deal about that planet's character. Pluto was discovered in 1930 at the time of the Great Depression, organized crime, the rise of Hitler—but also the rise of psychoanalysis. In Roman mythology, Pluto (the Greek Hades) ruled the underworld. But let's not forget that all the riches of the world are hidden beneath the ground: gold, water, precious metals, oil, and fossil fuels. Pluto rules wealth and is the god of hidden treasures and hidden talents. On a personal level, our own riches and resources are buried in our unconscious. When Sigmund Freud was asked the definition of psychoanalysis, he replied, "Making the unconscious, conscious." That's a perfect description of Pluto.

In mythology, Pluto was a dark and menacing figure who rarely ventured above ground; one of the rare times he did was when he kidnapped Persephone, brought her to the underworld, and made her his queen. Her mother, Demeter (the Roman Ceres), was bereft. As she was the powerful goddess of the harvest, she refused to allow anything to grow: no food, no flowers, no babies, no birds. The land remained frozen and barren. As a result, the other gods demanded that Pluto return Persephone.

Eventually, a deal was struck, and Persephone was allowed to return to the "day" world. When she came before Zeus (the Roman Jupiter and king of the gods), he asked her if she had eaten anything down below; as in the underworld, there are strict rules with dire consequences.

Persephone was a smart gal and knew the ropes. She told Zeus that she had not consumed any food during her captivity, but that just before she left, Pluto had shoved a pomegranate in her mouth, and she had swallowed some seeds. It's always the little details that get us in the end. Those seeds changed everything. She was allowed to stay above ground for only half the year; the rest of the time, she had to remain in the underworld with Pluto.

According to the Greeks, this is how the seasons originated. When Persephone was with her mother, the earth flourished, and we have spring and summer; when she was below and her mother grieved, it was fall and winter. But there is a deeper story.

When written in Chinese, the word "crisis" is composed of two characters.
One represents danger and the other represents opportunity.
—President John F. Kennedy

Whenever the planet Pluto appears, the ground shifts, our world cracks open, and life as we know it collapses. The planet of "extreme home makeover," Pluto destroys in order to rebuild. But it's not all doom and gloom. A very important part of the story is that Persephone found her true power and became a whole person in the underworld. She may have gone down an innocent girl, but she returned a queen.

There are other versions of the myth that suggest that Persephone ate some pomegranate seeds of her own volition so that she could remain connected to her new identity and power. Ultimately, this myth teaches us that buried within each crisis is an opportunity, and every death brings new life.

Thank God for Saturn

Nothing in life or in nature is meant to stay the same; at this stage of life, we are supposed to experience a situation that forces us to examine our life. This is why Saturn is so critical. If we've done the necessary work at our Saturn Return (taken on a challenge, worked hard, and matured in the process), then we have developed the ego strength and emotional muscle to navigate this part of the journey.

Not Everyone Will Experience a Major Crisis: A lot depends on the quality of our lives and the choices we've made thus far. If we're unhappy, frustrated, and living a lie, then the consequences and the crises will be greater. If we feel pretty good about ourselves and our lives, then what surfaces will be less dramatic. Remember, the planets don't *cause* the problems; they simply expose them. As the poet Rumi says, "The pot drips what's in it."

The Pluto Process: Pluto is always an invitation to look deeply and sincerely at what scares us and to have the courage to confront it. Whatever has wounded us that we haven't dealt with tends to surface at this time. It may involve a death—not necessarily a literal death but the death of some part of us, the ending of an old life. It may look like a current situation (we get involved in another abusive relationship, get fired from another job), but generally it refers to an older, deeper issue (perhaps with a parent or authority figure) that the current situation triggers.

Pluto's arrival signals that we are ready to deal with something that we couldn't handle before. We must make our own journey into the underworld (the unconscious) to reclaim those buried parts of ourselves. It is a kind of soul retrieval, a dark night of the soul, or, in the words of poet T. S. Eliot, "A condition of complete simplicity (costing not less than everything)." To its credit, Pluto often brings a guide to help us, frequently in the form of a therapist, spiritual mentor, or teacher.

The Shadow: What psychologists call the "Shadow" describes the unwanted and undesirable parts of our personality that don't fit the idealized image we have of ourselves. Banished to our unconscious, these disowned qualities don't cease to exist; they form a secondary personality. Then we find others to "carry" those parts for us.

For example, the woman who was raised to put other people's needs first and never express her own desires might be highly critical of those women who make their own needs a priority. Pluto has often been associated with the Shadow. This phase of the Midlife Journey is a time to connect with our Shadow. Embracing our Shadow allows us to move toward wholeness. As Carl Jung wrote in *Psychology and Alchemy,* "There is no light without shadow and no psychic wholeness without imperfection." We must make the best relationship we can with the worst parts of ourselves.

What Doesn't Work: Being arrogant, defensive, or in denial; blaming others instead of confronting our own issues and dark side. Jung said, "What is not brought to consciousness comes to us as fate." When we don't take responsibility for what is going on in our lives, we tend to keep attracting the same kinds of events and repeating the same old behaviors.

What Works: Doing deep psychological work: therapy, a shamanic vision quest, breath work, body work, Shadow work, recovery groups, or keeping a journal—anything that puts us in touch with our core issues and supports us working through them. We are birthing ourselves, and it's important to remember that the process is both painful and joyful.

In AA, they talk about "hitting bottom"—sometimes you have to lose everything before the healing can begin. As J. K. Rowling has said, "Rock bottom became the solid foundation on which I rebuilt my life." You can usually tell when someone has confronted his or her demons and has done honest Pluto work. Like a warrior returning from battle, she or he radiates a certain gravitas and humanity; they are fully present and comfortable in their skin.

Is Pluto Still a Planet?

Yes and no. In 1930, an American astronomer named Clyde Tombaugh discovered Pluto, and Pluto took its place as the ninth planet. Pluto didn't change, but in 2006, the definition of what constituted a planet did; Pluto no longer fit the definition. It was demoted to the status of a "dwarf planet" by the International Astronomical Union. However, astrologers continue to use Pluto and give it the respect it deserves. I suggest you do the same.

Pluto Types: People who have Pluto prominent in their charts (for example, their Sun is in Scorpio or in the 8th house, or Pluto is in aspect with a personal planet or angle of the chart) are intense, powerful, and often intimidating. They are the shamans, psychologists, and rescue workers—not afraid to face the dark side of life. They are also the politicians, power brokers, and drug lords.

How does someone become Plutonian? Not in a weekend workshop or graduate school. Often these people experienced an early loss or betrayal, had a near-death experience, or suffered some kind of trauma. Examples include Martin Luther King Jr., Oprah Winfrey, Hillary Clinton, the Dalai Lama, and Jack Nicholson.

Elisabeth Kübler-Ross—a Swiss-American psychiatrist, pioneer in near-death studies, and author of two dozen books—was born with her Cancer Sun in conjunction with Pluto. Her groundbreaking book, *On Death and Dying,* in which she first introduced her theory of the five stages of grief, was published in 1969 at the peak of her midlife. She didn't learn about the subject of death and dying in medical school—she was the one who introduced it! Kübler-Ross faced the topic while coming of age during World War II, then again later when doing her psychiatric residency in the United States, where she was appalled by the treatment of patients who were dying.

Pluto Wisdom: "Honest misery is far more energizing than perky dishonesty born out of defending something that wants to die." (Caroline Casey)

Robert Downey Jr.'s career really took off during his Saturn Return; he received glowing reviews for his work in movies such as *Air America, Soapdish,* and *Natural Born Killers,* and was nominated for an Academy Award as best actor for *Chaplin.* Unfortunately, his drug use took off as well.

Between 1999 and 2001, Downey was arrested dozens of times for drug-related charges. He bounced in and out of rehab. He even said to a judge at one point: "It's like I have a shotgun in my mouth, and I've got my finger on the trigger, and I like the taste of the gunmetal."

Then, during Downey's Pluto period (in 2002), after years of drug abuse, arrests, rehab, and relapse, something finally took hold; he made a full recovery and returned to his career. During an interview with Oprah in 2004, Downey talked about his addictive behavior and failed attempts at rehab. He told her that after his last arrest in April 2001, he knew he would be sent back to prison.

> I [finally] said, "You know what? I don't think I can continue doing this." And I reached out for help, and I ran with it. . . . You can reach out for help in kind of a half-assed way, and you'll get it, and you won't take advantage of it. It's really not that difficult to overcome these seemingly ghastly problems. . . . What's hard is to decide [to actually do it].[2]

In 2008, at the peak of his Uranus opposition, Downey starred in two blockbusters, *Iron Man* and *Tropic Thunder*. Finally, he was able to shed his reputation as a problem and a liability and receive acclaim and acknowledgment as a brilliant and highly respected actor. As of 2016, Downey has remained drug free, and his career has continued to flourish.

The Uranus Opposition

Midlife marks the time to begin cultivating whatever was
neglected during the first half of life.
—Carl Jung

The second phase or the peak of the Midlife Journey takes place between ages forty and forty-two, when change-at-all-costs Uranus, the planet of freedom, rebellion, and individuation, makes an opposition to its natal (birth) position.

---

[2]"The Comeback Kid," an interview with Robert Downey Jr., *www.oprah.com/oprahshow*

In Greek mythology Uranus, father of the Titans, was different from all other gods. He was not worshiped nor did he have shrines dedicated to him; instead, he represented and personified the sky itself, vast and limitless. Uranus was the first of the outer planets to be recognized; it was discovered in 1781, just after the American Revolution, before the French Revolution, and around the time of the Industrial Revolution.

Called the Great Awakener, Uranus is associated with what's new, different, or outside the mainstream; anything that challenges the status quo and questions authority. It is the planet of breakthroughs and discoveries of all kinds: scientific, technical, artistic, political, and personal—what Abraham Maslow called "peak experiences."

Uranus has been described as eccentric, electric, brilliant, a genius, an outlaw, and a troublemaker. This maverick takes roughly eighty-four years to return to its natal position, so between years forty and forty-two, Uranus reaches the halfway point. This signals that an old life is over and a new one is about to begin.

Around age forty, we begin to question everything we've been doing; we're restless, eager, and hungry for something we can't even name. Whatever we've put on the back burner during our Saturn years, while we're building a career or raising a family, begins to call out to us—sometimes quite loudly. The person who married early and never dated may suddenly crave freedom; meanwhile, the playboy or playgirl settles down.

At forty-one, Brad Pitt left his storybook marriage to Jennifer Aniston; he began a relationship with Angelina Jolie, started a family, and became increasingly involved in humanitarian work. Angelina filed for divorce from Brad Pitt in 2016 when she was forty-one. Carla Bruni, famous for her jet-setter life and rock star boyfriends (such as Mick Jagger), married French president Nicolas Sarkozy and became the first lady of France.

For many women, it is suddenly essential to get pregnant at this time. For instance, Salma Hayek, Halle Berry, Nicole Kidman, and Mariah Carey all gave birth for the first time between ages forty and forty-two. Other women decide to go back to school or return to the workplace. All of us experience a powerful desire to break free of some situation and find more meaning in our lives.

This can be a confusing time filled with self-doubt and uncertainty, but that comes with the territory; in fact, if we're *not* feeling like we're falling apart to some degree, then we may be out of touch with ourselves. This aspect has been called the Great Corrector; it is now time to question our choices, our direction, our dreams, and to make the necessary adjustments. If something isn't working in our lives or there's something we haven't explored or experienced, it can no longer be ignored. At midlife, we change our life, our "brand," sometimes even our sexual orientation. Secrets are told, the truth comes out, and lives are altered for better or worse.

Gail Sheehy published *Passages,* her record-breaking book about the adult life cycles, during her own midlife. Tina Turner finally divorced Ike. In 1988, at the age of forty-one, Larry David met Jerry Seinfeld, and together they wrote *The Seinfeld Chronicles,* which became the basis for the hit television show *Seinfeld.* During her Uranus opposition, in 1994, Oprah took a big chance; she changed her television format and moved from just being another tabloid talk show to one that inspired and uplifted. Ellen DeGeneres came out publicly as a lesbian during her midlife. In 1996, Steve Jobs (at age forty-one) returned to Apple, took control of that company, and brought it back from near bankruptcy to profitability. Chaz Bono underwent female-to-male gender transition.

Between 1999 and 2005, cyclist Lance Armstrong won the Tour de France seven consecutive times. However, in 2012, at age forty-one, he was exposed for having used illicit performance-enhancing drugs and was subsequently banned from competition. The following year, at the last contact Uranus made, a documentary called *The Armstrong Lie* was released, putting his story back in the spotlight.

The Uranus Process: If we've done the Pluto work—digging deep, facing our demons, and coming to terms with our fears—then *authentic impulses,* rather than addictions and crazy schemes, will surface during the Uranus phase. The key is to separate our heartfelt desires from our phony impulses. And while the name of the game is change during this time, it's not about changing who we are; it's about *discovering* who we are.

A Clue: Between the ages of twenty and twenty-one, we experience our first Uranus square. It marks the end of adolescence and our entrance into young adulthood. It's a time to spread our wings and test the waters. This may be expressed in various ways. For some it means getting married and settling down; while for others it involves rebelling. For many, there's a strong desire to find something to believe in, especially if that cause or group clashes with our parents' beliefs. As Howard Sasportas wrote in *The Gods of Change,* "Finding a world view which differs from that of our family is part and parcel of finding our own identity."

Often, whatever we've ignored at our first Uranus square at age twenty-one is what calls to us at our Uranus opposition at forty-two. The person who married early and never really dated may feel the burning need to experiment. Someone who has been on an ambitious career path may suddenly discover a desire to get married, start a family, or travel the world. Take a look at what you were doing and feeling at age twenty-one; it can help you understand what's calling you in your early forties.

What Doesn't Work: Freedom-loving Uranus doesn't do well with taking orders, so there's a tendency to rebel and act out. But looking *outside* provides only temporary change and excitement; going *within* is the inescapable necessity.

The cartoon version of a midlife crisis is the man divorcing his wife of twenty years, buying a motorcycle, dying his hair, and taking up with a young exotic dancer to regain his lost youth. There are plenty of examples from real life, in the tabloids or on TV. Jesse James, who was married to Sandra Bullock, didn't begin acquiring motorcycles and tattoos at forty-two; he already had plenty of both. His Uranus opposition simply exposed his relationship with a porn star, and that quickly put an end to his marriage.

What Works: Several years ago, Elizabeth Gilbert (author of *Eat, Pray, Love* and *The Signature of All Things*) was on *Oprah*, and she said something I have never forgotten: "Ask yourself every day, what do I really, really, really want?" She stressed "three reallys." That's a great question at any time in our lives, but especially during this phase.

At its best, Uranus is associated with clear-sighted experimentation and independence. You find something you really want, and you take the risks to make it happen. You may look crazy to others, you may get a lot of negative feedback, but it's essential to be true to yourself. During this time, we may feel as if we're living in Starbucks, overcaffeinated and overstimulated; it's important to channel that energy in a positive way. Some action is necessary; even small changes and baby steps are helpful.

Uranus Types: These are people who have their Sun in Aquarius or in the 11th house or who have Uranus making an aspect to a personal planet or angle of the chart. They are the rebels, the outsiders, the outlaws, and the geniuses who aren't afraid to think—and live—outside the box, to challenge authority and say "no" to power. They are the ones who bring something unique and original to the world. Examples include Sigmund Freud, Walt Disney, Steve Jobs, Steven Spielberg, Bono, and Oprah Winfrey; all of them have Uranus making a close aspect to their Sun.

Uranus Wisdom: "Before the beginning of great brilliance, there must be chaos. Before a brilliant person begins something great, they must look foolish to the crowd." (I Ching)

Neptune
Water wears down rock.
—truism

Around this same time, between ages forty-three and forty-four, Neptune enters the picture and makes a square to its birth position. Neptune was discovered in 1846. During that time, ether was introduced as an anesthetic, photography was developed, and the world saw the rise of Spiritualism and séances. Neptune is pure consciousness and is associated with spirituality, dreams, visions, and music, as well as illusion, deception, and addiction.

Pluto is deep and intense; it can shake us at our core. Uranus strikes like lightning; it's sudden and unexpected and can turn our life upside down. Neptune is subtle and silent, yet deceptively powerful; it erodes slowly, washing things away. During a Neptune period, we often feel a deep longing to connect with something greater than ourselves. It is a time for getting in touch with our inner life, exploring a spiritual path, or becoming involved with a cause. It can also be a time of sacrifice, for we must relinquish certain dreams while trying to find a new vision for our future. It's not unusual to feel lost, confused, and adrift; that's Neptune's way of slowing us down.

The Neptune Process: One of my favorite words is *sabbatical.* It's longer than a vacation, and it's paid for! I think we should all be able to take a long and leisurely sabbatical during midlife, similar to a maternity leave. Unfortunately, for most of us that isn't possible, but we do need to carve out time—down time, soul time, dream time, time to empty out, recalibrate, and evaluate.

What Doesn't Work: Using drugs, alcohol, food, TV, or the Internet to escape, as well as being too busy, constantly overscheduled and over extended, which is another form of distraction. AA suggests that during the first year or two of sobriety, one should not jump into a new relationship, change careers, or make major changes. The same goes for midlife. A time of confusion is not a good time for action. Of course, this isn't the only thing that is going on, but it's necessary to make space for Neptune's energy.

What Works: Three things: *surrender, surrender, surrender.* Neptune asks us to feel, dream, and listen loudly. Slow down, meditate, and spend time in nature. Keep a dream journal, explore Jungian therapy, paint, or listen to music.

This is not a time to overthink or analyze. Any process or activity that takes you out of your "monkey mind" and into the numinous can be helpful; especially anything that uses symbols such as Tarot cards, Nordic runes, the I Ching, or astrology.

There was a time not too long ago when stores weren't open on Sundays; there were no computers, cell phones, or iPads. Today information is coming at us 24/7; we watch war on TV, shop around the clock, and, thanks to social media sites, we are connected to thousands of people we don't even know. Our culture values action, speed, and results. There is not a lot of support for slowing down, tuning out, and turning inward.

That's Neptune's realm, and sometimes it is really necessary to go there. If we don't do it, we often find less conscious ways to slow down—for instance, getting sick, fired, or addicted. All of these are low-level responses to the need for more solitude and stillness in our life.

In his delightful book, *The Art of Stillness: Adventures in Going Nowhere,* author Pico Iyer writes about the beauty of slowing down. He notes that many people in Silicon Valley observe an "Internet Sabbath," turning off their devices from Friday night until Monday morning.

My friend Karol, who entered the convent when she was eighteen, taught me about the "Grand Silence." It begins at dinner and continues through breakfast the next morning. "We [she and the other young nuns] all knew how to talk, but we didn't know how to listen," said Karol. "You only find your own voice when you listen. Until you know your own voice, you don't know God's voice or even your own intuition."

Could you create your own form of Sabbath or Grand Silence? Could you live for a day or even an hour or two without checking your email? It doesn't necessarily have to be a weekend; start with a day or an evening. If you find you can't, then perhaps this is something you need to do.

Neptune Types: People with a strong Neptune have the Sun in Pisces, in the 12th house, or with Neptune in aspect to a personal planet or angle in the chart. They are artistic, dreamy, intuitive, and compassionate; they are the visionaries, musicians, poets, healers, artists, addicts, and fanatics. Michelangelo, Chopin, Edgar Cayce (the Sleeping Prophet), Frida Kahlo, Johnny Cash, and Kurt Cobain are a few examples.

Neptune Wisdom: "We need to return to the solitude within, to find again the dream that lies at the hearth of the soul." (John O'Donohue, *Anam Cara: A Book of Celtic Wisdom*)

I've heard people say that astrology doesn't work; it contradicts itself. Well, guess what? So do we. We're all a mixed bag: brave in some areas and panicked in others; capable of being both generous and mean-spirited. Life isn't tidy; it's complex, messy, and marvelous all at the same time. So is midlife. These different planetary transits overlap; that's part of the reason it is such a dynamic period.

Pluto has the power to expose our deepest fears. Thanks to Uranus, we can feel as if we're mainlining double espressos. Simultaneously, Neptune's influence feels as if we're under a spell and can't move off the couch or let go of the remote! Pluto, Uranus, and Neptune operate differently, but all three are trying to peel away whatever isn't authentic and wake us up to who we really are.

Even cowards can endure hardship; only the brave can endure suspense.
—Mignon McLaughlin

The key is to create space for all the various energies. During midlife, we need to learn to live with paradox, and part of that is being able to tolerate the unknown. In her wonderful book *When Things Fall Apart,* Pema Chodron wrote about the importance of becoming comfortable in that unsteady place: "The healing comes from letting there be room for all of this to happen: room for grief, for relief, for misery, for joy." If you are not familiar with Chodron and are going through midlife, then this is an ideal time to become acquainted with her work.

Enter Saturn: Phase Three

At age twenty-nine, we experience our first Saturn Return; twenty-nine years later, at fifty-eight, we have our Second Saturn Return. Around age forty-four, we've reached the middle point between the two returns: Saturn is opposite its natal (birth) position.

Remember, Saturn is a "do something" planet and works best when it is manifesting a project or a plan. There is a strong desire at this time to create something real in the world, or if we're already doing it, then to bring it to the next level. A couple things can happen. If we have made good choices during our Uranus opposition and had the courage to go for something we truly want, then Saturn helps us to anchor those choices in the world and integrate them into our life. In a way, Saturn "locks them in." Our mid- to late forties is a power time, and this is often a period when we receive recognition for what we've been creating.

Here are some examples: John F. Kennedy became president; Bill Clinton declared his candidacy for president. In 2000, at the peak of his midlife, Bono announced the formation of an organization to advocate debt relief for the Third World. In 2005, during his Saturn opposition, Bono scored a major victory at the G8 Summit (where the eight richest countries met); an agreement was forged to cancel forty billion dollars' worth of African debt.

It's no surprise that Barack Obama's Saturn is in ambitious and demanding Capricorn. He graduated from Harvard (magna cum laude) at his Saturn Return, published his memoir, *Dreams from My Father* (at thirty-four) and at thirty-five (at his opening Saturn square), he was elected to the Illinois Senate. In 2002 (at the peak of his midlife), he commissioned a poll to evaluate his prospects in a 2004 U.S. Senate race. In March of 2004, Saturn made an opposition to its natal position; he won by a landslide. In July 2004, he gave the keynote address at the Democratic Convention which made him a rising star, but the truth is he had done the necessary Saturn work.

If we haven't done the work or made any positive changes, then this can be a time of frustration. In fact, at this stage, we often become aware of how we have failed. That's not such a bad thing, since becoming conscious of something is the first step toward changing it.

No-nonsense Saturn demands accountability, so it's back to square one. It may be hard, and it may feel lonely, but if we are honest, humble, and willing to do what's necessary, Saturn will support us. Remember, we all have our own individual timing; as they say in AA, "It takes as long as it takes." You make peace with where you are; you begin again and again, if necessary, and continue moving in the direction of your dreams.

Midlife is not for sissies. It takes tremendous stamina and courage, not to mention compassion for yourself and for the entire scary, sacred, and miraculous process. Ultimately, it's worth it, for it is the deepest work we can do; it is soul work. As Jungian analyst and author James Hollis wrote in his book *Finding Meaning in the Second Half of Life,* "Your Self is seeking itself."

Jupiter Makes an Appearance at Age Forty-Eight

This special Jupiter Return comes during our forties, at a time when we are typically at the height of our powers. This is often a time when we buy a home, make an important investment, or find ways to reward ourselves. If we are still struggling, the wisdom planet can bring mentors and teachers, who can be influential, and ideas that can motivate us.

Putting It All Together

What did you do as a child that made the hours pass like minutes? Herein lies the key to your earthly pursuits.
—Carl Jung

Carl Jung's story is a great example of the Midlife Journey. In fact, Jung was the first psychiatrist to recognize this phase and write about it. In his late thirties, Jung experienced a major breakthough in midlife. Jung had been Sigmund Freud's protégé and the heir to the psychoanalytical movement; however, Jung was a rebel and a mystic, who used astrology in his practice, studied alchemy and mythology, and believed in the power of dreams. He could not go along with all of Freud's theories; Jung had to be true to himself, even though severing ties with Freud was considered career suicide at the time.

Jung's actions had repercussions, both personally and professionally, and he was shunned by most of his colleagues. In his book *Memories, Dreams, Reflections,* Jung wrote: "After the parting with

Freud, a period of inner uncertainty began for me. It would be no exaggeration to call it a state of disorientation."

Jung fell into a depression. Rather than go into therapy, he created his own method of treatment; he cut back on seeing patients, and every day after lunch he would spend time in his garden playing with his childhood toy soldiers. Jung remembered that as a young boy, this had given him enormous pleasure, and he used it as a way of reconnecting with something that he had lost. In the evenings, he painted and wrote in a large journal that he called *The Red Book*. He did not turn away from his inner turmoil; rather, he dug deep, he wrestled with his demons, and over time he healed.

Jung's Uranus opposition (at age forty-one) gave birth to his most important contributions: the discovery of the archetypes and his theory of individuation. As he wrote in *Memories, Dreams, Reflections*:

> The years when I was pursuing my inner images were the most important in my life—in them everything essential was decided. It all began then; the later details are only supplements and clarifications of the material that burst forth from the unconscious, and at first swamped me. It was the *prima materia* for a lifetime's work.[3]

Under this same transit, artist Georgia O'Keeffe discovered New Mexico and began spending a part of every year there, finding inspiration under the hard, blue southwestern sky and the whispering ponderosa pines. Laurie Lisle wrote in her biography

---

[3]C. G. Jung (ed. Aniela Jaffé), *Memories, Dreams, Reflections* (New York: Vintage Books, 1989), p. 199.

of O'Keeffe: "'The world is wide here,' she said about New Mexico in her old age, 'and it's very hard to feel it's wide in the East.'"[4]

During O'Keeffe's Saturn Return at age twenty-nine, she had her first exhibit in New York City, gained a reputation as an artist, and met and married the photographer and modern art promoter Alfred Stieglitz. Although her career was thriving, *something* was still calling her. New Mexico became her spiritual home, her creative muse, and the place with which she would ultimately become so deeply identified.

In 1919, at his Uranus opposition, Albert Einstein (then age forty) received validation for his theory of relativity, bringing him worldwide fame. Two years later, he was awarded the Noble Prize for physics. Other examples include Bill Wilson, who, after years of debilitating alcohol addiction, finally achieved sobriety and cofounded Alcoholics Anonymous. Rosa Parks refused to leave her seat on the bus in Montgomery, Alabama, and became the face of the Civil Rights movement. Betty Friedan published *The Feminine Mystique* and launched the modern feminist movement.

> *Anything or anyone that does not bring you alive is too small for you.*
> —David Whyte, "Sweet Darkness," *The House of Belonging*

Since how we navigate this period will determine the second half of life, the stakes at midlife are high. Get it wrong, and either we act out some adolescent fantasy and run the risk of throwing away a marriage or a career, or we do nothing and resign ourselves to a life that's no longer relevant. Get it right, and we're not so much running *away from* something as *going toward* it; we break out

---

[4]Laurie Lisle, *Portrait of an Artist: A Biography of Georgia O'Keeffe* (New York: Seaview Books, 1980), p. 220.

of a rut, go for something we really want, and we're rejuvenated in the process. If we've made the right choices, then ultimately we're not different from who we once were; we're more authentic and real. Or, as they said in Erhard Seminars Training (est), "I used to be different; now I'm the same."

Midlife Rituals

When a planet is in your life, the god or goddess represented by that planet is also present. It behooves you to honor that divine energy and get to know it. Suggestions: Create an altar to the planet; learn about the period in history when it was discovered; explore its mythology.

The 1991 film *City Slickers,* starring Billy Crystal and Jack Palance, is the ultimate midlife story. A group of male buddies, all of whom are having midlife crises, go on a cattle drive in the Southwest. They face their worst fears, are pushed to their limits, humiliated, and ultimately transformed. You don't necessarily have to go on a cattle drive, but breaking out of your routine, experiencing something new, different, and difficult is the goal.

For instance, take a bicycle trip through France, hike the Appalachian Trail, volunteer at an animal shelter, do a mediation retreat, or sign up for a writing seminar to jump start that novel you've been dreaming about—anything that shakes you up, wakes you up, and gets the juices flowing.

The Outer Planets

Uranus, Neptune, and Pluto are referred to as "outer planets." These distant spheres are too far away to be seen with the naked eye and therefore weren't discovered until we had telescopes. They govern our fate, destiny, and search for meaning.

They also move very slowly, so they occupy the same sign for years and have a lot to do with the generation to which we belong. Because of their slow pace, when they connect to a sensitive point in our charts, they hang around for a while—just to make sure we get the message and do the work.

Uranus by Any Other Name

In his book *Cosmos and Psyche,* cultural historian and philosopher Richard Tarnas makes an excellent case for Prometheus being a more suitable name for this unpredictable planet. In his opinion, and many astrologers agree, numerous talents and gifts associated with Uranus (sudden changes, spiritual awakening, inspiration, and brilliance) describe Prometheus perfectly. A true rebel and trickster, Prometheus was the Titan who sided with Zeus against Cronos/Saturn and the other Titans. It was Prometheus who stole fire from the gods to give mankind; a brave move that cost him dearly.

Location, location, location! Up until Uranus was discovered, Saturn was the outermost planet; naming the new planet after Saturn's father makes sense in terms of locality and linage but not in terms of temperament. In mythology, Uranus (Ouranos) was not known for qualities such as rebellion and liberation, but having been universally accepted, he is now associated with those traits.

Pluto's Orbit

Pluto, the slowest of the outer planets, has an erratic orbit, moving sometimes slowly and then quickly through the signs. In fact, midlife used to begin in our early forties, when Uranus made an opposition to itself, and Neptune squared itself, followed by Saturn's opposition to itself. But then Pluto sped up and joined the party; in fact, it has been throwing the party!

My generation (the Pluto in Leo gang, born 1937–1956) experienced the Pluto square at ages thirty-nine to forty. The Pluto in Virgo cohort (born 1958–1972) experienced it at thirty-six or thirty-seven, which means many of you had to deal with heavy issues at a younger age! Pluto is currently moving more slowly again as it travels through Capricorn; those of you born after 1972 will get the Pluto square at around age forty.

Transitions

In his inspiring and deeply moving book, *The Way of Transitions: Embracing Life's Most Difficult Moments,* author William Bridges wrote about the difference between change and transition.

Change is the action that takes place; we change careers, move cross-country, get divorced or married, or have a child.

Transition is the process of coming to terms with change, releasing the way things used to be and adapting to the new way they become. If we don't take the time for transition or if transition is interrupted, then change is not complete, and nothing is really different. According to Bridges, transition is a three-phase process: there is an ending, then what he calls the neutral zone, followed by a new beginning.

Midlife is about transition, and navigating the neutral zone is the key to getting it right. It feels like we are in limbo or what the

Jungians call "liminality." I call it the "hallway," as in, "One door closes and another one opens, but it's hell in the hallway."

However, I have found that it's also "holy in the hallway." Magic happens. You're sitting in Starbucks and discover a magazine with an article that is life changing. Or you have a conversation with someone on a train that sends you in a totally different direction. The neutral zone is a very fertile place, filled with pure potential for those willing to hang out there.

My Midlife Journey

When I was growing up, my mother was fragile and childlike but able to function. Over the years, she began to withdraw more and more; then in her early fifties, she had a serious breakdown. The diagnosis was schizophrenia. Thanks to medication and my father's care, she was able to remain at home. Occasionally, and always in the middle of the night, I'd wonder: What if something happened to my father, who was thirteen years older than my mother, and I had to take care of her? What would I do? How would I manage? My mother was only sixty-seven and not physically ill, but she required supervision.

I didn't think about it all the time, but the possibility lurked in the background. It was my own worst fear. Then it happened. My father suffered a stroke in the summer of 1981. Upon release from the hospital, he went into a nursing home. From the time I was in my twenties, I had supported both of my parents financially and otherwise, but now I had full responsibility for my mother. This was different; this was daunting.

Simultaneously, I was breaking up with my boyfriend, who also happened to be managing my restaurant. Oy vey! Rob had a background in restaurant management and had brought a level of professionalism to my business—or so I believed. Not only was I devastated at being dumped, I was panicked that my staff would walk out with him when he left. Every area of my life was collapsing at the same time. I was living on coffee, running on empty, scattered, and scared as hell.

My parents lived in Great Neck, Long Island, about twenty-five minutes from New York City. Every day I would drive out to check on my mother, to make sure she took her medications and had her meals. Eventually, I hired someone to stay with her during the day, then someone else to be with her at night, but it was still a lot to handle.

On many days, I would drive further out on Long Island to the nursing home to visit my father. This was before the Internet, and there was very little helpful information about elder care; I was really out of my depth. I remember crying in the car while driving to Long Island, crying in the office at my restaurant, crying myself to sleep at night while I prayed what Anne Lamott calls "beggy" prayers: making deals with saints and gods I had only a passing acquaintance with.

The summer passed, then fall. I found someone I trusted to live with my mother full time. My father was still in the nursing home but not doing well. It seemed as if he might die at any moment, so naturally I never took any time off from visiting him. Then one weekend, Stewart Emery was in town doing a seminar; he was the creator of Actualizations, a group whose work I'd been very involved with during the seventies. Initially, I thought that the seminar could be an opportunity for Rob and me to heal our relationship. Yes, I was still hanging on to that relationship, and Rob was still running the restaurant. I'm a double Taurus, and change is not my specialty. It takes the "jaws of life" for me to let go of anything.

I convinced Rob to attend the workshop with me. I was concerned about taking the time to go, but at that point it had been several months since my father's stroke. What were the chances there would be any changes that weekend?

On Friday night, I arrived at the workshop, which was held in a midtown hotel. The lights dimmed for a meditation as Pachelbel's Canon began playing softly in the background. This music has always brought me to tears, and I immediately started to weep. I found myself saying, "I love you" to my father.

When I was a teenager, he'd been extremely abusive and violent toward me, but I had long ago forgiven him. At the hospital, I often told him I loved him, but it wasn't really real, if you know what I mean; I didn't *feel* it. That night was the first time I meant it. The workshop was powerful for me, but it didn't help my relationship with Rob. He and I broke up for real.

I came home with a splitting headache. I remember getting into a hot bubble bath and sitting in the tub for a long time, ice pack on my head and a glass of vodka nearby, as the tears poured out of me. I went over everything: my relationship, the restaurant, my parents—the entire trauma and drama. Then I started thinking: I know I'm no saint; I'm not easy, I'm insecure, I'm nuts, but I'm not a bad person. I've worked on my issues; I've tried to do the right thing. This went on for quite a while with many refills of hot water and bubbles. I finally said to myself, "You know what, I really like myself. In fact, *I love myself*." Wow! That was the first time I was able to say that—ever.

The next day, Monday, I arrived at the restaurant early to do payroll. The first thing I saw was a message on my desk from the hospital (this was before cell phones and texting) to call immediately. It turned out that my father had died on Sunday. It felt as if he'd been waiting—not only for me to say I loved *him,* but also for me to say it to *myself.* My first Uranus square (which took place between ages nineteen and twenty) was when I ran off to Europe. I had tremendous anger toward my father, toward men in general, and most of all toward myself. This Uranus period had healed that.

I was desperate to find a new manager, and a friend in the restaurant business gave me some valuable advice. "Look around your restaurant and find the most competent person, preferably a woman. It doesn't matter who; it could be the hat-check girl, a waiter, dishwasher, whoever. Hire her and train her."

That's exactly what I did. Susan was an assistant chef, a good worker, responsible, and had leadership skills. She became my manager, and she stayed with me until I sold the restaurant thirteen years later. As for my fear that the staff would all follow the boyfriend out the door? It was a nonissue. I got my restaurant back and found my power. Most important of all, I faced my worst fear and survived.

By the time of my Saturn opposition, the restaurant was doing really well, and for the first time I started to make money. I bought a house out on the East End of Long Island, a dream come true. It really was the beginning of a whole new chapter of my life.

Stories
Janice's Story

Janice worked as a court reporter for twenty years; seven in family court and thirteen in the Supreme Court. Sure, it's nerve-wracking; in fact, a court reporter is the second most stressful job in America; the first is air traffic controller. But the pay is excellent, there's a great pension, and you have a chance to make a ton of extra money selling transcripts to lawyers.

"*Nobody* ever leaves that kind of job security," Janice told me. She actually enjoyed the work and loved the security, but eventually the stress got to her. "Going to work on the subway every morning, I would sweat so much I had to stand between the cars to get some air." She gave her boss notice and left on her birthday. She was forty years old and having her Uranus opposition. She went on to become a successful health professional and eventually a shaman and healer.

Susan's Story

My manager, Susan, was really smart, capable, and very loyal. But with her Leo Sun in the public 10th house, she really needed to be working for herself. I sometimes felt as if she were *my* boss! At the peak of her midlife, she met her future husband, married, and got pregnant immediately. I was just beginning to study astrology, but I remember telling her, "This isn't just about having a baby; with Uranus also hitting all the angles of your chart, I think this is going to influence your career."

Susan had a terrific voice and loved to sing but didn't want to pursue it professionally. Once her daughter was born, she learned about a program to teach singing to children. She started as a teacher, then bought her own franchise and ended up being successful at it. It brought all of her skills together in work that gave her a lot of joy.

THE CHIRON RETURN
The Youth of Old Age (Ages 49–51)

Forty is the old age of youth; fifty is the youth of old age.
—Victor Hugo

Between ages forty-nine and fifty-one, Chiron (a minor planet associated with the myth of the Wounded Healer) returns to its natal or birth position, and we officially take leave of our youth. It is a time to make peace with ourselves, come to terms with our failures, and forgive ourselves for what we haven't accomplished. Some old dreams have to be sacrificed, yet like an exquisite evening gown that can no longer be worn, the material may be used to make something new.

Chiron was discovered in 1977, around the time the word "healing" became a buzzword. That same year, *A Course in Miracles* was published, Louise Hay wrote her first book (*You Can Heal Your Body*), and the Omega Institute for Holistic Studies in Rhinebeck,

New York, opened. It would become one of the nation's most popular and trusted retreat centers. All three of these events began quietly, yet over time, they would prove significant. Each in its own way energized the growing trend toward more holistic types of treatments and body/mind therapies, while simultaneously generating questions about the traditional forms and mindset of Western medicine.

The Human Potential Movement was spreading, and practices such as Transcendental Meditation and personal growth seminars like est (Erhard Seminars Training) were at their peak. It was a time of enormous self-discovery. Alcoholics Anonymous began back in 1935, but it wasn't until the late seventies and early eighties that 12-step programs such as Adult Children of Alcoholics and Overeaters Anonymous came into being. In many ways, Chiron himself was the original Adult Child of Alcoholics.

In Greek mythology, Chiron was a centaur (half man, half horse), simultaneously mortal and divine. Chiron was the offspring of Saturn (the Greek Cronos) and a sea nymph named Philyra. In one story, Philyra turned into a horse in an attempt to escape Saturn's rape. In another version of the myth, it was Saturn who transformed himself into a horse when his wife, Rhea, discovered him with Philyra. Regardless of which parent took equine form, Saturn didn't stick around to see his son grow up; Chiron's mother was repulsed by him and refused to have anything to do with him.

Rejected by both of his parents, Chiron retreated to a cave where he raised himself. There he was mentored by Apollo (the Sun god) who taught him healing arts such as homeopathy, herbs, and natural medicine, as well as astronomy and astrology. Athena (the goddess of wisdom) was also one of his tutors.

As a result, Chiron became a gifted teacher and healer; the kind who brings out the best in his pupils. His students included Jason,

Hercules, Achilles, and other sons of great men and gods. Chiron taught them to be the heroes they were meant to be. The Chiron Return teaches us to be heroes—not who or what we thought we were but who we truly are.

Every age with a zero is daunting, but none more than the big 5-0. The fifties are an exciting time once we actually arrive; but the approach can feel unnerving, especially if we're not happy with the life we have. There is something about turning fifty that just screams for us to stop pretending: pretending to be happy, satisfied, and, above all, pretending that it's okay to be taking caring of everyone else and ignoring our own needs.

At fifty, we have to drop the mask we've been showing to the world and not worry so much about what others think. This can be both freeing and frightening. It can also be particularly challenging if we're strongly identified with a role that has outlasted its usefulness yet comes with certain perks attached.

Some people cannot or will not make the transition. It's not uncommon for people to die around this age: Judy Garland, photographer Diane Arbus, Michael Jackson, Whitney Houston, to name a few. This decade of one's life has a "grow or die" quality. As the poet Rainer Maria Rilke wrote: "For here there is no place that does not see you. You must change your life."

Change Your Story, Change Your Life

Wounding becomes sacred when we are willing to release our old stories and to become the vehicles through which the new story may emerge into time. When we fail to do this, we tend to repeat the same old story over and over again.
—Jean Houston

At our Chiron Return, we have the power to change our story, and it isn't unusual for our life to take off in a new direction. In our late forties and leading up to the Chiron Return, there's a significant period where ideas, plans, and projects are seeded. Since Chiron is located between the orbit of Saturn (a visible planet that represents tradition) and Uranus (a distant planet that is associated with progress and freedom) it's frequently referred to as a *bridge,* because it links the old and the new.

It's not uncommon for a teacher or mentor to appear at this time, who acts as a bridge or catalyst from one life direction to another. At other times, a failure or a loss can serve as a catalyst. Sometimes it can be both. Pay attention, because many seemingly ordinary meetings and events take place during the period leading up to the Chiron Return that ultimately can be life changing.

In her late forties, Jackie Kennedy Onassis surprised the world by taking a job as an editor at Viking Press. The vehicle for that move was Letitia Baldrige, who had once been Jackie's social secretary at the White House. She knew of Jackie's great love of books and suggested she consider a career in publishing. Baldridge encouraged Jackie to contact editor and publisher Tom Guinzburg of Viking Press. Jackie took her advice, called him, and accepted a job as a consulting editor. A year later, she moved on to Doubleday. The world of publishing provided a necessary sanctuary for Jackie during that period of her life. She would ultimately edit more than one hundred books.

During her late forties, supermodel Lauren Hutton spent much of her time in self-exile. Then photographer Steven Meisel featured her in the now-famous Barneys New York ad, in which she was not made up to look like her younger self but was allowed to appear as her own age. Hutton became the poster girl for women over fifty. She also revived her modeling career and paved the way for older models.

In her late forties, after the death of her great love (Denys Finch Hatton) and the loss of her beloved coffee plantation in Kenya, Karen von Blixen Finecke, better known by her pen name Isak Dinesen, returned to her native Denmark where she began writing. At fifty-two, she published her memoir *Out of Africa*.

Rejected by her publisher, the manuscript of Julia Child's book, *Mastering the Art of French Cooking,* landed on the desk of a young assistant editor at Knopf named Judith Jones. As luck, destiny, or synchronicity would have it, Jones was passionate about French cooking. She took the manuscript home and tried out some recipes. Jones saw the book's potential and convinced her boss to publish it. At age forty-nine, having finally published her famous book, Julia Child left France and returned to the States; nine months later, she launched her brilliant television career—one that spanned three decades.

Just as in the fairy tale *Sleeping Beauty,* it sometimes takes another person or an event to awaken a dormant part of ourselves. The Chiron Return can do that for us. Without Letitia Baldridge, Jackie Kennedy Onassis might never have considered a job in publishing. Likewise, had it not been for Judith Jones, Julia Child's manuscript might have remained buried in the rejection pile.

Assuming her career was over because of her age, Lauren Hutton initially refused that groundbreaking modeling assignment. Yet Steven Meisel wouldn't take "no" for an answer, and finally she agreed. However, when Hutton arrived at the photo shoot wearing jeans, a work shirt, and no makeup, Meisel recognized something in her and, through his photography, was able to bring it to the surface. Isn't that what a great Chironic teacher or therapist does?

Chiron and Health

Our bodies can act as catalysts by sending messages to us in the form of symptoms. So it's not unusual for health issues to surface at this time, for both men and women. This is not meant as a prediction and obviously does not occur for everyone; it's just one of the many ways Chiron can manifest.

Louise Hay wrote her first book, *Heal Your Body,* in 1976 at her Chiron Return. Around the same time, she had been diagnosed with incurable cervical cancer. She rejected conventional medicine and instead cured herself through a program that included forgiveness, therapy, and nutrition. Her book, which began as a small pamphlet, was later expanded into *You Can Heal Your Life* and was published in 1984 at Hay's Second Saturn Return at age fifty-eight. Louise Hay, along with her bestselling book, is a great expression of Chiron, himself a great healer and teacher.

In 2010, Dr. Mehmet Oz, who was then fifty, was diagnosed with polyps during a routine colonoscopy. He had the procedure done as part of his TV show (*The Dr. Oz Show*). Afterward, Oz said that the procedure had probably saved his life. He used his crisis to serve as an opportunity to bring awareness to the issue of colon cancer and encourage others to get tested.

I've heard it said about Chinese medicine that we are born with a certain amount of *chi,* or energy, that stays constant until around age forty-eight or forty-nine. After that, we need to refine our habits. For those of us in good health, this may involve small adjustments, such as eliminating wheat or dairy, getting more sleep, changing our exercise routine, or adding certain vitamins. On the other hand, if we haven't been paying attention to our health, then this is the perfect time to get serious about it.

One of the most positive things we can do for ourselves at this particular passage is to get a full medical checkup. Integrative medicine is a growing trend that includes the best of both mainstream medicine and alternative therapies that treat the whole person. Since Chiron was a healer who worked with natural remedies, it may be timely to explore such treatments as acupuncture, homeopathy, and Chinese herbs.

Chiron and Menopause

With our child-rearing years behind us, our creative energies are freed. Our search for life's meaning begins to take on a new urgency, and we begin to experience ourselves as potential vessels for Spirit.
—Christiane Northrup, MD, *The Wisdom of Menopause*

Unlike other cycles, the Chiron Return is accompanied by real biological changes, as it coincides with the median age of menopause in women; in the Western world, that age is fifty-one.

"Menopause" comes from the Greek root words meaning "the cessation of monthly cycles." But perimenopause (*peri* means "around" or "near") can begin at around forty, when many women experience some bone loss and hormonal changes. Astrologically, that is the same time as the Uranus opposition, a time of waking up to who we are. By age forty-four, most women begin to have irregular periods and 80 percent skip periods all together. By the late fifties menopause is usually complete, which means that the entire process goes from midlife to the Second Saturn Return.

At menopause, our hormone levels are changing, and it can feel as if our filters have disappeared. Emotions bubble up, nerves are raw, tempers explode. Whatever needs and desires we've repressed for the sake of keeping peace and maintaining the status quo break through to the surface. Sometimes it isn't pretty, and although the timing may be wrong and we overreact, it's important to remember that the *emotions themselves are real.* Change is inevitable, and our hormones are the key to getting in touch with that. Christiane Northrup notes that this is the time when our hormones give us an opportunity to see—at last—what were need to change in order to live fully into the second half of our lives.

> *"No" is a complete sentence.*
> —Anne Lamott

Problems occur when we don't make the necessary changes, when we stuff our emotions down and don't express our feelings. Then our bodies find ways to get our attention, sometimes creating serious illnesses. In *The Wisdom of Menopause* (probably the best book on this subject), Christiane Northrup writes that menopause demands an outlet. If it doesn't find an outlet, a voice, a way to express itself, then what can break down is our health. The result can be one of "the big three" diseases of postmenopausal women: heart disease, depression, and breast cancer.[5]

Northrup wrote about menopause not as a collection of symptoms that must be fixed or eliminated, but about the transformation that is available at this time. Today, people are living and working longer. This period of life is an opportunity to establish a new level of health and well-being, one that will sustain us in the years ahead.

According to Northrup, it depends on two things. "First, we must be willing to take full responsibility for [our share of] the

---

[5]Christine Northrup, MD, *The Wisdom of Menopause* (New York: Bantam Books, 2006), pp. 9–10.

problems in our lives. . . . The second requirement for transformation is more difficult by far: we must be willing to feel the pain of loss and grieve for those parts of our lives that we are leaving behind."[6]

During her Chiron Return at fifty-one, Gloria Steinem discovered a tiny lump in her breast. She immediately went for a mammogram and it proved to be benign; a follow up test also proved negative, and she accepted the results without question. Another test, the following year, revealed it was malignant. Steinem chose to have a lumpectomy and underwent six weeks of radiation treatments.

By her own admission, the only exercise she got at this time was running through airports; Steinem worked constantly, ate poorly (often consuming large quantities of ice cream), and her apartment wasn't properly furnished; it was merely a place to change clothes between business trips.

Around this same time, a close friend encouraged Steinem to see a therapist. For all her brilliant accomplishments, influence, and energy, Gloria Steinem had never explored her childhood and its extreme poverty and lack of parenting. The therapy opened a window into her past and gave her the tools to heal. She slowed down and began to take better care of herself.

Another friend helped her furnish the apartment, teaching her the value of fine cotton sheets. Afterward, she wrote *Revolution from Within: A Book of Self Esteem,* which was published in 1992, at her Second Saturn Return. Behind the beautiful face and fierce drive that she presented to the world was a vulnerable little girl with enormous self-esteem issues.

Perhaps one of the rewards of aging is a less forgiving body that transmits its warning faster—not as a betrayal,

---

[6]Ibid, p. 11.

but as wisdom. Cancer makes one listen more carefully, too. I began to seek out a healthier routine, a little introspection, and the time to do my own writing, all of which are reflected in these pages.[7]

Joan Anderson married young, raised a family, and had a career as a journalist and author. When she was around fifty, her husband got a job in Chicago, so they sold the family home in New York State. She then shocked both of them by deciding not to join him. Instead, she took a vacation from her marriage and role as mother and caregiver to spend time alone at their cottage on Cape Cod. Her book, *A Year by the Sea,* is the story of her year of self-discovery and her journey back to herself.

Jungian analyst and author Jean Shinoda Bolen had separated from her husband of nineteen years and was going through a period of uncertainty when she received in the mail a mysterious envelope from a complete stranger. (This is exactly the kind of synchronicity that so frequently occurs during our Chiron Return.) Inside was an invitation to go on a spiritual pilgrimage to Europe in search of the sacred feminine. This journey led to a spiritual awakening and her exquisite memoir, *Crossing to Avalon.*

While women, thanks to science, are giving birth later in life, there is still something deep in our psyche that knows that this period is indeed the end of our fertility. For past generations, menopause signaled the end of being a woman. In 1900, the average life expectancy for females around the world was about forty-five, so many women didn't even experience menopause; the ones who lived past that age were considered *old.* We carry those stories in our cells.

---

[7]Gloria Steinem, *Revolution from Within* (Boston: Little, Brown and Co., 1992), p. 246.

Although there is much to celebrate during this period, there is also much to mourn, and we need to make time to do that. We may no longer be able to have children after fifty, but in many ways, this is our time to give birth to ourselves and to create lives that reflect the person we have become.

At the same time that women are going through menopause, men are having their own version—male menopause. Often referred to as andropause or "man-opause," it is associated with a slow, steady decline of testosterone. The symptoms are not as dramatic as for women but can include nervousness, depression, fatigue, insomnia, and sometimes even hot flashes and sweats. While women are looking to the outer world (the workplace, creative projects, or returning to school) to satisfy their emerging drives, men are often drawn more toward family and the home.

With goals, hormones, and lives all changing, it's no surprise there are so many divorces between people in their early fifties. If there are problems in a relationship, then they will most likely surface during this period; relationships don't necessarily have to end, but they may need to be renegotiated.

> *The Chiron Return is a major threshold crossing, where the past is transformed in our attitude to it, and we can experience a new beginning, often with a renewed sense of the spiritual dimension of life.*
> —Melanie Reinhart, *Chiron, Pholus, and Nessus: To the Edge and Beyond*

The Wounding and the Healing
The Chiron Process

The Chiron Return takes us back to whatever has not been healed, and it is not unusual for difficult memories and traumas to surface. These are often connected to family patterns that have continued for generations. Let's face it; there are some things we're just not ready to look at until we're fifty and have experienced our share of losses, betrayals, and disappointments. Something within us seems to soften at this age and allow us access to the necessary wisdom and compassion.

In her book *Chiron and the Healing Journey,* Melanie Reinhart writes about the Greek word *kairos.* "The word means opportunity, the right moment, when the timeless . . . nature of an experience may suddenly reveal itself, releasing a process which was previously frozen or stuck; a dam may give way, enabling the river of our life to continue flowing." The Chiron Return is an excellent time to enter therapy or embark on a spiritual practice, but it's important to remember that this is not an intellectual process. It is less about analyzing or fixing and more about *healing, embracing, and forgiving.* We can seek help, but ultimately at our Chiron Return, we must heal ourselves; the change must come from within.

Chiron was wounded a second time when his student Hercules shot him with a poisoned arrow by mistake. With all his wisdom and skills, he could not heal himself; and because he was immortal, he could not die. Chiron was finally released from his suffering by a strange twist of fate. It was Hercules who pleaded with Zeus to allow Chiron to trade places with Prometheus, who was being punished for stealing fire from the gods to give to the mortals. Prometheus was freed and because of Chiron's willingness to sacrifice himself, he was allowed to die. Zeus immortalized him as the constellation Centaurus. And so the wound was healed by the very one who had caused it.

What Works: In Greek mythology, Chiron was known for his compassion, so the most powerful thing we can do at this time is to let go of the tyranny of perfection and the habit of comparing our insides to the botoxed, airbrushed *outsides* of others. We do that by loving ourselves for who we are and not for what we do or have. This is not ordinary self-love; *it's radical self-love, radical self-forgiveness, and radical self-acceptance.* I'm not suggesting this is easy; it's a lifetime process. But for those of us who are hard on ourselves (and sometimes others) and who have not forgiven ourselves (or others), the Chiron Return is a gateway into rectifying this.

The ancient Hawaiian prayer *Ho'oponopono* means: "I'm sorry, please forgive me, I thank you, and I love you." I can think of no better metaphor or message for the Chiron passage. By making peace with ourselves, our past, and the people in our lives, we are liberated to live more freely and fully in the years to come. That is the great gift of the Chiron Return.

What Doesn't Work: Unresolved issues, old traumas, and shame do not just disappear; they fester. When they are not dealt with, they can lead to addictive behavior or chronic illness. The Chiron Return is the ideal time to work on these issues, and compassionate mentors and healers who can help us often come into our life.

The wonderful thing about our fifties is that we're old enough to have acquired experience, skills, and some wisdom, but still young enough to do just about anything. Okay, well, maybe not become an Olympic ice skater or a prima ballerina, but there is still so much ahead of us. In fact, there is no other period in our lives when we have both a wealth of experience on one hand, and on the other a significant amount of time to create something of value. What a fabulous place to be.

The biological calendar has been reconfigured so that people
are physically younger than their chronological age. This has
created a whole new stage in the life cycle—a period of personal
renaissance inserted somewhere after middle age but before old age.
—Abigail Trafford, *My Time: Making the Most of the Bonus Decades after Fifty*

Chiron Rituals

Even more than during other cycles, we need down time, soul time; time to mourn, digest, and process old wounds and the portion of life that is coming to an end. The feelings and memories that need to surface can only do so in a quiet and safe environment.

Even if we don't do formal meditation, taking time to be still or walk in nature helps us to process. Consider a ritual that involves the burning of some old relic or old love letters. Go through old photos, throw some out, and create a photo album with the rest. Or visit a childhood place. Participating in a shamanic journey, pilgrimage, or spiritual retreat can be profound at this time. Or do a simple full moon ritual during which you write a letter to the old self you are leaving behind.

A Bathrobe Day

Bathrobe days are always a treat, but they are especially helpful during a Chiron period. For me, it's the perfect way to unwind, tune out the world, and reconnect with myself. I give myself permission to do anything I want or absolutely nothing at all. Sometimes I stay in bed, reading my favorite magazines or a juicy novel. There is usually a bubble bath involved, naps, and great snacks. No guilt or inner critics allowed.

Chiron Types

People with Chiron prominent in their charts are often healers, teachers, mentors, or the heroes who bring a new vision for the future. Like Chiron, they may have been orphaned, wounded, rejected, or sacrificed by their family or by society.

Martin Luther King Jr. and Mahatma Gandhi both had a prominent Chiron and both used nonviolence to communicate their message. Barack Obama's Chiron is in the first house; he is very much associated with the mythology of this planet.

Saturn Square between Ages 51 and 52

An important change developing here introduces seven years in which more and more the answer to your problems will be found within yourself, less and less in the outer world.
—Grant Lewi, *Astrology for the Millions*

The closing Saturn square comes at the end of the Chiron Return; in fact, they overlap. It can feel confusing at times; the Chiron experience is profound and emotional. Saturn's arrival brings reality and responsibility. It's necessary to make room for both energies. Saturn is the scaffolding, the framework on which we construct our life. That includes the stories we repeat to ourselves and others. We may have outgrown certain aspects of ourselves, yet our outer life may not reflect it; during this time, we have the ability to bring them into alignment.

As we move toward our Second Saturn Return, it is not so much building as eliminating and consolidating.

The Progressed Lunar Return at 54

At age twenty-seven, we experience our first Progressed Lunar Return, which lays the groundwork for our Saturn Return at twenty-nine. Now, twenty-seven years later, we have another; this one is the harbinger of our Second Saturn Return at fifty-eight.

During our twenties, our reference points are our parents and their values; those values begin to alter as we get in touch with who we are and what we want to create in the world. At fifty-four, there is another shift—one less centered on the outer world and our responsibilities and more about our inner life and what makes us happy.

The Moon is our mood, our emotions, and, just as we did at twenty-seven, we get a *feeling* about who we will become at our Saturn Return. We are pregnant with something, and if we tune in, we can feel the stirring of a new life forming. It is a listening time, a learning time.

The Moon contains immense amounts of information about who we are on the deepest level. It is our emotional life and origins, even what we experienced in the womb. Breaking old patterns are easier now, especially those based on the demands of others.

In her book, *Chiron and the Healing Journey,* Melanie Reinhart wrote about how we are reparenting ourselves during the first few years after the Chiron Return that coincides with the Progressed Lunar Return. At the same time, we may be dealing with our aging parents and still have children living at home. It's no surprise that issues around family and parenting surface. This can be a deeply healing time if we give ourselves permission to explore and process these emotions.

Two Filmmakers, Two Films, Two Chiron Stories
The Edge of Dreaming

Documentary filmmaker Amy Hardie experienced a loss, an illness, and, ultimately, a healing at her Chiron Return; along the way she changed her story and her life. Amy is a science filmmaker who lives in Scotland; she has a beautiful family and work that she is passionate about. One night, she dreamed that her beloved horse died; the next morning, she woke to find out it was true.

Shortly afterward, just before her forty-eighth birthday, she had another dream in which her late partner, the father of her first child, told her she would die within a year. Racing against the clock, she set off to research dreams. In the beginning, she took a purely rational and scientific approach. Later that year, she was diagnosed with a rare lung disease, and medical tests showed that she had only 60 percent lung capacity. She spent time in a hospital, but the medical world couldn't help her. Only after visiting a shaman in Edinburgh was she finally able to heal and to celebrate her forty-ninth birthday.

The Edge of Dreaming is a deeply personal documentary that shows Amy at every stage of her journey; at home with her family, learning about the death of her horse, her search for help via the medical community, and the session with the shaman.

What struck me about her story was that it contained many symbols connected with Chiron. Chiron himself was half horse; horses are associated with shamanism. Like the planet Chiron, the horse represents a bridge between the visible world of form (Saturn) and the distant world of the unknown and the unseen (Uranus). Amy went from being someone who made scientific-type films (she has worked with stem-cell researchers) to researching death for a documentary set in a hospice.

I Am

Tom Shadyac, the Hollywood director of such mega hit movies as *Ace Ventura: Pet Detective, The Nutty Professor, Liar Liar,* and *Bruce Almighty,* was living a life most of us can only imagine. His home was a seventeen thousand square-foot mansion, he flew on private jets, and he went to A-list parties with Hollywood royalty. Yet he experienced a sense of emptiness.

"I was standing in the house that my culture had taught me was a measure of the good life," Tom recalls in his documentary *I Am*. "I was struck with one very clear, very strange feeling: I was no happier."

In 2007 (at the age of forty-nine), he had a traumatic bike accident that resulted in excruciating post-concussion syndrome. It was so horrific that he began to welcome the thought of death. "Facing my own death brought an instant sense of clarity and purpose," he says in his film. "If I was, indeed, going to die, I asked myself: What did I want to say before I went? It became very simple and very clear. I wanted to tell people what I had come to know. And what I had come to know was that the world I was living in was a lie."

Two burning questions led him to begin filming *I Am* just five months after his accident. "What's wrong with the world, and what can we do about it?"

The film *I Am* is a series of conversations with some of our most profound and respected thinkers, such as David Suzuki, Noam Chomsky, Colman Barks, Archbishop Desmond Tutu, and Lynne McTaggart. Shadyac began a quest to discover what would make him happy and to find out what is wrong with the world. As a result, he changed his lifestyle dramatically.

He traded his mansion for a modest mobile home, chose to bike to work, and now flies commercial. He says in the film that he's never been happier. "I started to wake up to certain hypocrisies in my life about ten or twelve years ago, and I started shifting things as I asked [myself] more and more questions. . . . The bike accident is what compelled me to share my journey."

My Chiron Return

By 1988, I had owned my restaurant in Greenwich Village for fourteen years, and it was doing really well. After many years of working double shifts and doing just about everything from bussing tables to baking and bookkeeping, I had a solid staff and some freedom; I was even making money. Plus, a few years earlier, I had bought a house on Long Island and finally had time to spend there. Life was good. Then I went and opened another restaurant. Oy vey! What was I thinking?

I had wanted to open a second restaurant for quite a while, but the restaurant business is hard and lonely, and I was concerned about taking on another one by myself. My sister suggested that we open one together in the Berkshires (in western Massachusetts), where she lived, which was about three hours away from New York City.

In the town of Great Barrington, we found an old coffee shop and renovated it. It was my dream restaurant; it had red oak floors, wainscoting, and Laura Ashley wallpaper. It was twice the size of my place in Greenwich Village, and it even had a bar. While we were jam-packed in the summer (the Tanglewood Music Festival, Kripalu Yoga, and Canyon Ranch were all nearby), business *died* during the winter. Needless to say, I hadn't done any market research. I poured all my money into trying to keep it going. Meanwhile, I was going back and forth on the train every week and had no days off or down time. It was just like the early days, except now I was older, had more to lose, and I was frightened instead of fearless.

Then something interesting happened, which often does in those years leading up to the Chiron Return. I became friends with a woman whom I met in Great Barrington. She and her husband lived in Manhattan but had a weekend home in the Berkshires, and I would often drive back to the city with them on Sunday nights.

One evening, on our way back, my friend read out loud from an astrology book; it was Steven Forrest's *The Inner Sky*.

Steven's book was a revelation. His language was poetic, and his images profound; he described the planets, signs, and houses in a way that brought them alive. I borrowed the book and saw that my friend had written his phone number in the back.

I called Steven for a natal reading, then for another that covered what was currently going on. My life was falling apart, but those couple of hours on the train each week going up to the Berkshires were like gold; I listened to my taped readings or read astrology books by authors such as Liz Greene and Howard Sasportas. A whole new world was opening up for me; a world of mythology, magic, wisdom, and inspiration.

I closed the restaurant in the Berkshires in the fall of 1990. Back in the city full time, I struggled to keep my original restaurant going; it had always been popular, but the economy in the early nineties still hadn't recovered. The restaurant needed new equipment, such as an air conditioner, but I no longer had the funds. I began looking around for a buyer.

At the same time the restaurant was winding down, my interest in astrology was growing. I began studying astrology and attending astrology conferences. I wasn't thinking of it as a career; it was something I loved, so I embraced it. The fact that it wasn't contaminated by any of my problems or financial pressures was a welcome relief.

In the fall of 1994, during the peak of my Chiron Return, I experienced a series of losses; my mother died, my beloved cat Tasha died, and the restaurant hit bottom. I finally realized that I just couldn't do it anymore and decided, buyer or no buyer, I would have to close. I set a date in late February 1995, so all the loyal customers would have a chance to get their final piece of peanut butter ice cream pie or warm gingerbread with fresh whipped cream.

The *New York Times* did an article about the restaurant closing; not only were we busy, but a buyer came through at the last moment. I was able to pay all my bills and had enough money left over to live for a few months.

I felt absolutely lost and completely disoriented. For twenty years the restaurant had been my life, my identity, and my community. I didn't know who I was without it. I remember walking home one night after spending the day cleaning out the restaurant once it was closed.

"Dear god," I remember thinking, "I'm too old to be a waitress. What in the world am I going to do now?" I wish I could tell you it was a smooth transition, but it was pretty ragged and involved several part-time jobs and many false starts. I'm not only a late bloomer; I'm also a slow learner. So it took me a while, but little by little a new life began to unfold.

Jubilee Year

There is a decree in the Jewish faith that every seven years the land is to lie fallow. This fallow year is known as a *shemita* year Seven shemita years make forty-nine—the same age as the Chiron Return. The fiftieth year is a Jubilee or sabbatical year. During this holy year, each person is returned to his ancestral heritage, debts are annulled, and any Jewish person in slavery is released. In the Cabala, the number seven is considered sacred. It can also refer to Saturn, as every seven years, Saturn makes an aspect to its natal position.

Traditional Hindu Society

In the Hindu tradition, there are four stages of life. The first is the Student (Brahmacharya), from ages twelve to twenty-four. The second is the Householder (Grihastha), from twenty-four to forty-eight. The third is the Elder Advisor (Vanaprastha), from forty-eight to seventy-two, which takes place at the Chiron Return. At this time, a man has fulfilled his responsibilities as a husband, provider, and family man and may retire from secular life alone or else lead a life of contemplation and meditation together with his wife. The final stage is Renunciation (Sannyasa), from seventy-two onwards.

Stories
Uggie

Uggie is the name of the Jack Russell terrier who received raves and an honorary Oscar for his performance in *The Artist.* Uggie was rejected by his first two owners and was on his way to the dog pound when Omar Van Muller took him home as a foster dog. Von Muller, a dog trainer, noticed that Uggie was smart and willing to work, so he began training him. He has had several roles, but his big break was *The Artist.* He was fifty years old in dog years and having his own Chiron Return at the time.

Lauren's Story

Lauren was divorced at forty-three, at the peak of her midlife. That's also when her life began to unravel. Lauren was a talented artist, textile designer, and jewelry maker who lived in upstate New York. Financial pressure forced her to close her design studio and dissolve her business.

She found a job in retail, but (at forty-five) she tore a ligament in her foot, and it was difficult to stand. She quit her job. She sold her beloved loom, the rare silversmith tools handed down from her father, and other possessions. Her daughter went to live with Lauren's ex-husband, which Lauren found heartbreaking. Finally, she just couldn't support herself. Her sister offered her a refuge in Brooklyn; just a tiny room with no window, but it was a sanctuary—a place to rest and recover. She was utterly exhausted.

It was during her Chiron Return that she began to heal. After several months of "recovery," Lauren decided to look for work. Due to her design background, she was able to get a job selling luxury Tibetan rugs at a high-end department store. The situation wasn't perfect, but she stayed there for a two and a half years and learned as much as she could. She appreciated the beauty of the rugs and discovered that she was really good at selling them; plus, she found that she could make excellent money.

Based on that experience, she landed a position in another store, again selling rugs. Lauren moved into her own apartment. She was able to help support her daughter, who was now in college. For a while, Lauren's mother came to live with her until Lauren could find a suitable assisted living facility. Lauren even began to make art again.

She is now stronger and happier than ever before. "I just couldn't get it together financially. I didn't know what a goal was. Having goals totally changed my life. I can make plans now; I have options. This period broke an old pattern."

Karol's Story

At eighteen, Karol joined the Sisters of the Holy Cross. One of the benefits of becoming a nun is the education that's available. Karol completed her BA (in sociology), then her master's degree in theology.

In her mid-forties, she took a two-year sabbatical from St. Mary's College (Indiana), where she was dean of students, to come to New York City and complete her PhD in higher education administration at NYU. St. Mary's was grooming her to be president, thus the need for the PhD. While in New York, Karol realized that she didn't want to return to South Bend, Indiana, and work as a college administrator.

Karol had already published several books, and what she really wanted was to remain in New York City and write. It was a huge decision; she had been a part of the Sisters of the Holy Cross for thirty-three years. Around this time, she was diagnosed with a fibroid tumor. She remembered reading that fibroids were caused by blocked creative energy. That settled it.

It was during her Chiron Return that she made the decision leave the order and remain in New York. She didn't give up her vows; she joined the Sisters for Christian Community, which is a contemporary, self-governing organization whose members live independently. Karol went on write several more books and never looked back.

THE SECOND SATURN RETURN
The New Elder (Age 58)

Wisdom is one of the few things in human life that does not diminish with age.
—Ram Dass

At age fifty-eight, there's another shift as we enter the phase of the elder. Once again, taskmaster Saturn is our guide when we come to our Second Saturn Return. And you thought you were finished with the Saturn Return. Sorry, it returns every twenty-nine years.

Before you mutter Dorothy Parker's famous "What fresh hell is this?" let me explain. Yes, it's the same old "tough love" Saturn we met at twenty-nine, so it involves discipline, responsibility, commitment, reality, and new challenges. With our first Saturn cycle as the reference point, we've outgrown ourselves again; we need a new purpose, a great work—one that will occupy the rest of our lives. But at this age, our goals are different, and so are we.

During our first Saturn cycle at age twenty-nine, we're invited to move from youth to adulthood; at age fifty-eight, during our second Saturn cycle, we move from adulthood to becoming an elder. During the first cycle, it's normal to be self-centered; we're establishing an identity and carving out a place for ourselves in the world. At that age, the ego runs the show, and we tend to be driven, competitive, single-minded; we're focused on what we want to *get*.

In the second cycle, the ego is no longer in charge; it's more about what we want to *give*. What kind of legacy do we want to leave? What do we have to offer the community? What kind of elder do we want to become? In our late fifties, the need to "make our mark" or "take the world by storm" recedes and is replaced by a growing desire for wisdom, self-knowledge, and transcendence. This doesn't mean we can't continue to be active, ambitious, and successful, but ideally, at this point in our lives, we're motivated more from a desire for *meaning* rather than simply for achievement and recognition.

What Is the Great Purpose for This Phase of Our Life?

There is a power rising in you and an invitation to give your gift to the world.
—Steven Forrest

Comedian Billy Crystal is a wonderful example of the Second Saturn Return. His career took off at his first Saturn Return when he appeared as Jodie Dallas on *Soap,* followed by *Saturday Night Live* and a string of major films.

During his Second Saturn Return, he wrote and starred in a successful one-man show on Broadway. He named it *700 Sundays,* the amount of time he had shared with his father, who had died when Billy was fifteen. This touching tribute is filled with Billy's trademark humor, but it's also deeply moving and bares the hallmarks of a high Saturn, the compassionate elder.

Author Frank McCourt began a brand-new career at his Second Saturn Return. He was fifty-nine and retired from teaching when he met Ellen Frey, the woman who would become his third wife. She encouraged him to finally put down on paper the stories he'd been telling to his cronies in bars and taverns; the result was his Pulitzer Prize–winning book, *Angela's Ashes,* which he published at age sixty-four.

If you've read this memoir or seen the movie about his bleak childhood in Ireland, marred by poverty, neglect, and near starvation, you know that it's a book he could not have written in his youth. The work that comes to us later in life is not that of a young person. Billy Crystal's one-man show or Frank McCourt's book required more than sheer writing or acting talent; loss, pain, tears, humility, and a lot of hard-earned life experience were necessary ingredients.

For some people, it's during this third act that they finally receive the recognition they deserve. The artist Cezanne had his first one-man show when he was in his late fifties. At fifty-eight, Al Gore was the subject of the Academy Award–winning documentary *An Inconvenient Truth.* At fifty-nine, Gore won the Nobel Peace Prize, a Primetime Emmy Award for Current TV, and was named runner up for *Time's* Person of the Year.

Hillary Clinton campaigned (the first time) to be president of the United States during her Second Saturn Return. She was appointed secretary of state shortly after that. Kathryn Bigelow won an Oscar for her film, *The Hurt Locker*—the first woman to win the Academy Award for directing. In 1982, at his Second Saturn Return, Jimmy Carter started the Carter Center, a nonprofit organization devoted to advancing human rights and alleviating human suffering.

We're not all famous people with high-profile careers, but we all need a way to be in the world as an elder person. Saturn is a no-nonsense planet and wants to manifest something real and finite—as well as something different for everyone. At our first Saturn cycle, we often find a mentor; at the second, we have an opportunity to become one. There's a desire to pass on what we know, to leave some tangible evidence of our existence, so this may well be the time when we begin to teach or consult in our chosen field.

This transition doesn't have to be professional in nature; for many people, it means being able to spend time with grandchildren, travel the world, become involved in philanthropy or volunteer work, or finally have the time to write the book that's been calling them. Others reinvent themselves and discover new energy in the process. What's important is that the projects we pursue and the life we lead reflect who we've become and not who we once were.

Both Leslie Stahl (television journalist and correspondent for *60 Minutes*) and author Anne Lamott (*Travelling Mercies, Bird by Bird*) wrote books about becoming grandmothers. Anne Lamott wrote *Some Assembly Required* with her son Sam Lamott. It was published when she was fifty-eight (at her Saturn Return).

Leslie Stahl was seventy when her first grandchild was born. Her book, *Becoming Grandma: The Joys and Science of the New Grandparenting,* came out in 2016. "This is what I didn't expect. I was at a time in my life where I assumed I had already had my best day, my tallest high. But now I was overwhelmed with euphoria," she wrote.

Andy Rooney worked for CBS for twenty-nine years (a full Saturn cycle), but it was in 1978 (when he was fifty-eight) that he began dispensing wisdom on the segment "A Few Minutes with

Andy Rooney" that appeared each week at the end of *60 Minutes.* He continued to do it until October 2011, a month before his death at age ninety-two. Andy Rooney accomplished many things in his life (journalist, author of *My War,* writer and producer of award-winning television documentaries), yet he is most remembered for this brief weekly segment.

What Does It Mean to Be an Elder?

What does it mean to be an elder in this culture? What are my new responsibilities? What has to be let go of to make room for the transformations of energy that are ready to pour through the body-soul?
—Marion Woodman, *Bone*

There's more to becoming an elder than simply aging. Turning fifty-eight or sixty doesn't place the mantle automatically on your shoulders. You may be a full-fledged member of AARP and have an abundance of success, wealth, or worldly power but still not have access to the many dimensions of elderhood.

As astrologer Steven Forrest says,

> Elder is an archetype; there's another archetype available; it's called an old fool. . . . The difference between an elder and an old fool is that we *want* to spend time with an elder; we can't wait to get away from the old fool. An old fool gives *unsolicited* advice; an elder gives *solicited* advice.[8]

Like "elder," the word "crone" is unpopular; it sounds positively archaic and definitely not relevant or sexy. Yet in ancient times, crones (like elders) were the wisdom keepers, healers, and shamans.

---

[8]Steven Forrest, from a class lecture, used with permission.

Women are generally associated with being crones, but "crone" refers to the feminine quality in both genders, so men qualify as well.

In earlier times, calling someone a crone was a great compliment. According to Jungian analyst and author Marion Woodman, the word crone means "crown," and it represents the pinnacle of a life lived as consciously as possible. On her CD, *The Crown of Age: The Rewards of Conscious Aging,* Woodman explains that we are born or *crowned* twice; once at birth and again when we become an elder.

Croning ceremonies are returning. Women in their fifties, sixties, and seventies are welcoming their maturity and celebrating it as a way to reclaim the once-honored standing of the crone. Traditionally, the ceremony takes place at age fifty-six (right before the Second Saturn Return), but it can be done as early as age fifty. Dancing, singing, poetry, guided meditations, and a celebratory meal are often included. So is taking a new name. But you can create your own ritual; what's important is to honor the past and acknowledge this new phase of life.

Another ritual for this cycle is to gather together a group of friends and read Jean Shinoda Bolen's book, *Goddesses in Older Women: Archetypes in Women Over Fifty.* Her book is filled with empowering advice and deep wisdom on how to be a juicy crone.

Let's be clear: at fifty-eight we *enter* the realm of the crone and the elder. The Second Saturn Return signals a major transition, but we are just at the beginning of this great phase; we are rookie elders, newbies, freshmen. Becoming a true elder or a genuine sage is a process—not an event—and that requires time as well as consciousness, compassion, and patience. As Marion Woodman says on her CD, "The goal is not perfection. The goal is wholeness." Fortunately, we have great role models, wise teachers and juicy crones who have come before us to show us the way.

From Age-ing to Sage-ing

In the introduction to his warm, wise, and inspiring book, *From Age-ing to Sage-ing,* the late Rabbi Zalman Schachter-Shalomi wrote about approaching sixty. On the surface, his life was extremely active and his work fulfilling; he was a rabbi, a scholar, a professor of religion at Temple University in Philadelphia, and a pioneer in a movement to renew Jewish spirituality in the contemporary world.

Yet when he was alone, he felt anxious and out of sorts. "A feeling of futility had invaded my soul, plunging me into a state of depression that no amount of busyness or diversion could dispel."[9] As a rabbi and spiritual leader, he was the one who provided the answers for others; yet when "I confronted my own aging process, I didn't know how to answer the new questions that life so insistently was bringing to my attention."[10]

Rabbi Zalman decided to go on a forty-day retreat at the Lama Foundation near Taos, New Mexico. Once he settled in, and the noise in his head receded, he was surprised to realize that he was being initiated as an elder, a sage. He let his intuition guide him as he instinctively began to look back on his life—as he began to do what he refers to as "harvesting" his life.

To initiate this process, he asked himself, "If I had to die now, what would I most regret not having done? What remains incomplete in my life?"[11] During his retreat, he spent time in meditation or prayer, wrote letters to his children, and ultimately gathered a new vision for what he termed *elderhood.* He returned with a fresh sense of enthusiasm and a commitment to making his vision real.

---

[9]Zalman Schachter-Shalomi, *From Age-ing to Sage-ing: A Revolutionary Approach to Growing Older* (New York: Warner Books, 1995), p. 1.
[10]Ibid, p. 2.
[11]Ibid., pp. 2–3.

Back home, he read extensively on gerontology and life extension; consulted with philosophers and researchers, such as Jean Houston and Gay Luce; and, most of all, studied his own eldering process. From his exploration, he founded the Spiritual Eldering Institute in 1987 and began conducting workshops around the country, dealing with the issues of eldering and aging. In 1995 (with coauthor Ronald S. Miller), he published *Age-ing to Sage-ing,* still one of the best books on the aging process.

What Rabbi Zalman discovered was a renewed purpose, one that was built on his years of being a spiritual leader but was now being shaped by his evolving needs and the needs of his community. Finding something to devote our lives to is part of the great journey of this cycle. Following Rabbi Zalman's example and giving ourselves some time to examine our life is a good place to begin.

Life Review

To know where we're going, we need to examine where we've been; a life review can give us that perspective. This concept was developed in the early 1960s by psychiatrist, gerontologist, and Pulitzer Prize–winning author Robert N. Butler. Butler is considered the founder of modern gerontology, and his pioneering work has since gained widespread acceptance and respect among psychologists, social workers, and gerontologists.

At age fifty-eight, the natural desire to sum up one's life makes the life review both an excellent ritual and a deeply healing process. It involves writing down events in our life, thus far, as a way to bring to consciousness the different stages of our lives and reintegrate any unresolved conflicts. The result can provide greater self-acceptance and self-compassion, both of which help us move forward.

A life review can be done alone, but it's more effective when done with another person or in a group. There's something empowering about sharing our story, especially out loud. Gene D. Cohen, MD, in his book *The Creative Age: Awakening Human Potential in the Second Half of Life*, wrote: "Sometimes it is only when we tell our whole story or get it down on paper that we are able to 'connect the dots'—literally connect the dendrites—to gain a meaningful view of ourselves and our lives."

In the theater, the Third Act is when everything that happens in Acts I and II must pay off if the play is to be memorable. "Maybe life is like that," I thought. Maybe, in order to know how to have a good Third Act, I needed to look back at Acts I and II—to do what is called a life review.[12]
—Jane Fonda, *Prime Time*

In *Prime Time*, Jane Fonda writes about her experience of doing a life review. At first she merely recorded events in chronological order, but that turned out to be dry and unsatisfying. By studying old photographs, speaking with relatives, and getting inside those experiences emotionally, she began to understand what had happened on a deeper level. She also discovered greater compassion both for herself and her mother, who had committed suicide when Fonda was twelve.

Fonda notes: "What the experience of doing a life review has taught me is that while we cannot undo what has been, we can change the way we understand and feel about it, and this changes everything."[13]

[12]Jane Fonda, *Prime Time: Love, Health, Sex, Fitness, Friendship, Spirit* (New York: Random House, 2011), p. 20.
[13]Ibid., p.36.

Retreats and Rituals

We can't all go on a forty-day retreat like Rabbi Zalman, but some kind of "time-out" is the perfect way to honor the Second Saturn Return. Retreat centers like Esalen (in California) or Omega (in upstate New York), as well as many destination spas frequently conduct weekend and week-long seminars on the subjects of aging and the second half of life.

Ron Pevney, author of *Conscious Living, Conscious Aging* and founder of the Center for Conscious Eldering in Durango, Colorado, wrote that "Life review is the foundation for much of the inner work of conscious eldering." His center offers a selection of programs for elders, conducted in retreats and spas around the country. Michael Meade (*www.mosaicvoices.org*) is a renowned storyteller, author, and mythologist who brings a fresh perspective to ancient myths and cross-cultural rituals. He offers lectures, conferences, and residential retreats for young and old alike.

You can also initiate this cycle with a meditation retreat, shamanic journey, or creative workshop. But you don't necessarily need a formal workshop or retreat center. Simply getting away from your usual routine and locale with the intention of exploring and "harvesting" this new phase of your life is beneficial. Consider creating a weekly or monthly support group to do life reviews or to share ideas, books, and articles on this new elder phase. An ongoing group can be a valuable source of support as you learn how to navigate this passage.

Rabbi Zalman believed that, in the future, the work in spiritual eldering would be conducted in residential retreat centers that combined the best of spiritual communities such as Omega and Esalen Institutes. The retreats would include training in life reviews, preretirement planning for people in midlife, programs for elders, and instruction for young people who want to apprentice themselves to conscious elders.

There would be colleges that include all ages. "By providing the communal support, the knowledge, and the spiritual technologies to school people in their depths, these centers will initiate people into the profound mysteries of conscious aging."[14]

The Inner Journey

In modern culture people try to change their outer appearance to look younger, but the role of the elder is to go deep inside, to stay in touch with the eternal as well as the sage in one's heart.
—Michael Meade

A recurrent theme in many of the books and lectures on aging is the need to develop our inner life as we get older. In his book *Finding Meaning in the Second Half of Life,* James Hollis wrote that there are two major tasks in the second half of life. "The first is the recovery of personal authority."[15] According to him, that means "to find what is true for oneself and to live it in the world."[16] The second task is "discovering a personal spirituality." He goes on to explain, "A mature spirituality will seldom provide us with answers, and necessarily so, but will instead ask ever-larger questions of us. Larger questions will lead to a larger life."[17]

In his essay, *The Four Stages of Life,* Carl Jung points out that we would not live to be seventy or eighty years old if this longevity had no meaning for the species. He used the analogy of the sun

---

[14]Schachter-Shalomi, *From Age-ing to Sage-ing*, p. 249.
[15]James Hollis, *Finding the Meaning in the Second Half of Life* (New York: Gotham Books, 2005), p. 183.
[16]Ibid., p. 184.
[17]Ibid., pp. 185–186.

passing through the sky from early morning to night to describe the aging process. Youth was "morning," midlife was "noon," and old age was "night time." He referred to the elder years (from fifty-six to eighty-three) as the "afternoon of life" and described it as "just as full of meaning as the morning; only, its meaning and purpose are different."

Jung believed that cultivating a spiritual outlook is what healed patients in the second half of life, and he recommended using contemplative tools such as dream analysis and creativity. Journaling, yoga, prayer, or spending time in nature are also ways to awaken those parts of the self that were not developed while we were building a career and constructing our social persona. Rabbi Zalman's experience endorses this by quoting Jean Houston: "When we don't have to devote a large percentage of our time in fulfilling social obligations and meeting other people's expectations, we can unleash these energies and harness them for self-awareness, spiritual development, and creativity."[18]

Meditation

If you correct your mind, the rest of your life will fall into place.
—Lao Tzu

The Canadian police do it. The folks at Google do it. The Bank of England does it. Paul McCartney, Jerry Seinfeld, and Lena Dunham do it too. And thanks to the David Lynch Foundation for Consciousness-Based Education and World Peace, between 70,000 and 150,000 students in 350 schools throughout the US and South America also do it. The foundation also teaches meditation to US military veterans, African war refugees, and prison inmates.

---

[18]Schachter-Shalomi, *From Age-ing to Sage-ing*, p. 34.

The practice of meditation is one of the best ways to quiet the mind and go within. Rather than withdrawing from the world, meditation helps us become more present and live more fully. Yogis have been meditating for thousands of years, and now hard science has caught up. Research shows that people who meditate have changes in the area of the brain associated with memory, thinking, and learning.

Meditation also reduces stress, increases levels of empathy, boosts creativity, and helps with depression. It doesn't seem to have any downside, and unlike most things in life, it costs nothing— *and* you can do it anywhere. There is Transcendental Meditation, Mindfulness Meditation, Hindu Meditation, Buddhist Meditation, Vipassana (also known as Insight Meditation), and even walking meditation. It doesn't have to be long, hard, or uncomfortable. Even meditating for three minutes a day can raise the quality of your life.

Meditation 1, 2, 3

1) Sit up straight. 2)-Follow your breath. 3) Empty your mind. When your mind wanders (because that's what the mind does), just restore your attention. Don't judge. Continue. Sharon Salzburg said that the most important moment [of your meditation practice] is when you remember to bring your mind back.

Pema Chödrön's book, *How to Meditate: A Practical Guide to Making Friends with Our Mind,* is a great introduction. The American-born

Tibetan Buddhist nun brings her gentle yet straightforward style to this ancient practice. Sharon Salzberg, Jack Kornfield, Jon Kabat-Zinn, Tara Brach, and Thich Nhat Hanh are all highly respected teachers of meditation and have many fine books, CDs, and videos on the subject; there are even apps. Deepak Chopra and Oprah Winfrey's 21-Day Meditation Experience is a popular program available online.

> But loving-kindness—*maitri*—toward ourselves doesn't mean getting rid of anything. Maitri means that we can still be crazy after all these years. . . . We can still be timid or jealous or full of feelings of unworthiness. The point is not to try to change ourselves. Meditation practice isn't about trying to throw ourselves away and become something better. It's about befriending who we are already.[19]

The potency of youth is defined by energy, strength, and speed; in our late twenties and early thirties, we are like the heroes of old, intent on conquering and changing the world. Our middle years are propelled by a need for leadership, accomplishment, and power. The gifts of age arise deep inside; it's the wisdom that we have acquired from distilling and integrating the various parts of our life and from the perspective that comes from living longer and seeing the big picture.

We may lose influence in the outer world and become less visible (this is especially true of women), but there is another kind of power that arises and new doors that open. By not being as competitive, we are more present and less threatening, which results

---

[19]Pema Chödrön, *The Wisdom of No Escape and the Path of Loving-Kindness* (Boston: Shambhala Publications, 1991), p. 2.

in greater respect and deference. As Michael Mead writes in his book, *Fate and Destiny,* "Elders have an inner authority developed by becoming the authors of their own lives and the bearers of a living destiny."

> *That's the whole meaning of life, isn't it? Trying to find a place for your stuff.*
> —George Carlin

Comedian George Carlin's famous routine about our "stuff" remains relevant because it's so true. We carry around a lot of "stuff"—material stuff as well as emotional baggage. Most people at this stage begin to give away their stuff. There's less and less desire to acquire and accumulate, and a need to scale down becomes stronger. With kids who are grown and moved away, many people naturally downsize; they move from a big house to a condo or begin thinking about a retirement community.

It's time to consider the next generations: to make our wills or update them, or, if one is wealthy, to set up trusts or endow a university—all excellent Saturn rituals. Even if we don't have a great deal of money or valuable possessions, we naturally begin thinking about *our stuff.* Who gets our favorite painting or jewelry? Who will take care of the cats when we're gone?

On her CD, *The Crown of Age,* Marion Woodman speaks of the need to simplify our lives, about the fact that as we get older we don't have the physical energy or the time to deal with a lot of unnecessary possessions; we need that energy for our spiritual life. It's a time to streamline and let go of whatever isn't vital and that includes relationships, situations, and activities that no longer energize us and are holding us back. "You want your resources for your strength, and your responsibility is to your spiritual strength," Woodman said.

Death Enters the Conversation

The secret of life is to die before you die.
—Eckhart Tolle

Years ago, while visiting my dear friend Marguerite Churchill in Lisbon, I had the opportunity to meet Conchita Citron, the great female bullfighter. Known as the "golden goddess," she began her career at fourteen and fought on foot and horseback.

Marg had become friends with Conchita in Hollywood in the 1940s when they were both young. Conchita was at the height of her career as a bullfighter; Marg was an actress who had starred on Broadway in *Dinner at Eight* before going to Hollywood, where she appeared opposite John Wayne in *The Big Trail* and two dozen other films.

Though I'd heard stories about Conchita for years, I didn't meet her until Marg moved to Lisbon, where Conchita also resided. Conchita was in her late fifties at the time, a small woman with a strong presence and impressive posture. We were having tea at Marguerite's charming apartment on Rua da Bempostinha, and between sips of Earl Grey, Conchita looked straight at me and asked with authority, "Do you think about god? Do you think about death?"

I was speechless and couldn't think of any response. She probably thought I was naïve at best or, more likely, a complete fool. She would have been right; I was in my mid-twenties and—to put it mildly—still asleep. "I think about both every day of my life," she announced proudly, breaking an awkward silence. I had absolutely no idea what she was talking about. I do now! Like Conchita, I think about God and death on a daily basis; not in a depressed way and not out of fear but as a natural part of life.

Something happens as we approach the threshold of sixty: death enters the conversation. It becomes something real, palpable.

You realize you're closer to the end of your life than you are to the beginning, and that awareness can deepen you and influence the choices you make. Being fully conscious of death doesn't diminish life; it enhances it and makes it more alive. In fact, death is so much a part of our existence that to deny it its rightful place is to negate life itself.

In his book, *Fate and Destiny*, Michael Meade wrote about how the ancient people placed death in the center rather than relegating it to the end of life, out of sight, so as not to have to deal with it. "Death used to be called the great teacher of life; for in knowing something about death people came to value life more distinctly. The point of considering the role of death in life isn't to be morbid; rather, facing one's own mortality may help clarify one's role in life."[20]

> *It is different because it has a ring of mortality—*
> *so it has a big message of stop wasting time.*
> —Gloria Steinem, *Doing Sixty and Seventy*

At our Second Saturn Return, we realize we simply don't have all the time in the world, and that's not such a bad thing. Personally, I don't want to do everything, have everything, or be everything. When I was younger and owned the restaurants I could multitask like a pro—cooking, ordering, bussing tables, doing the books, etc. Now I hate the idea. I just want to focus on what's important—period. Life is short; so is my Bucket List.

What happens if I get ill? Where will I live in ten or twenty years? How do I want to spend the precious time I have left? In this economy, many people are postponing retirement; in some cases,

---

[20]Michael Meade, *Fate and Destiny: The Two Agreements of the Soul* (Boston: GreenFire Press, 2010), p. 218.

it isn't an option. Whether you retire or keep working, these questions need to be discussed. They become very real at our Second Saturn Return, and part of becoming an elder is a willingness to deal with them.

An advance directive is a general term that describes a document, often including a living will, in which a person makes provision for medical treatment in the event that they are not able to communicate their decisions to a doctor. Just talking about the end of life, let alone filling out a medical directive, can be intimidating. My friend Irene solved that by organizing a gathering at her home on this subject. About a dozen people showed up.

Irene invited two professionals to answer questions and help people with the forms; her good friend Laurie who had been a nurse for many years, and another friend, Judith Redwing Keyssar, a registered nurse, palliative care director, and author (*The Last Act of Kindness: Lessons for the Living from the Bedside of the Dying*). Everybody had lots of questions about the legal aspects but also the physical and emotion side of it. Some people chose to fill out the forms there, others decided to do it at home; but they all left with more information and less fear about the whole process. This is a wonderful idea and a perfect ritual for the Second Saturn Return.

Death Cafés

What in the world is a death café? Well, it's not as scary or strange as you might think. People simply gather in cafés or living rooms, drink tea, eat cake, and discuss the end of life. There is no charge and no staff; it is run on a purely volunteer basis. The aim is talk about death (along with grief, loss, wills, and burial rites) in a safe and respectful environment. This concept is based on the work of Swiss sociologist, Bernard Crettaz.

In the UK in November 2010, John Underwood read about Crettaz's work in a newspaper article and opened the first Death Café. This franchise spread quickly, and there are currently over 1,000 cafés all over the world. What's interesting is that this whole concept caught on while Saturn (the planet of seriousness) was in Scorpio (the sign associated with death and taboo subjects).

Gen Xers and Millennials are creating their own ways to deal with grief, loss, and bereavement. The Internet is full of blogs, websites, Instagram feeds, and YouTube series by people in their twenties and thirties, bringing the conversation out in the open, which is where it belongs. These Gen Xers and Millennials are helping us all have a better relationship with death.

Role Models

What we all need, whatever our age, are personal role models of living in the present—and a change that never ends.
—Gloria Steinem

My friend Marguerite, whom I mentioned above, was one of my greatest role models. When we met in Rome in the early sixties, I was just nineteen. Marg was in her fifties, drop-dead gorgeous, feisty, funny, and outspoken. She was also an avid reader (she devoured a book a night), a world traveler, a gourmet cook, and she could repair, restore, and sew just about anything.

When I was growing up, my own mother was ill, and I had to become the parent. Marg was not only a role model but the mother I never had; her home became a refuge.

When she was sixty, she relocated from Rome to Lisbon. A move to another country with a new language is daunting at any age, but Marg pulled it off and made a life there. She had always loved music but never formally studied. In Lisbon, she found a teacher and began seriously studying the viola; the viola became her late-in-life passion.

We're living in an aging society. As a result, there is more research, information, and inspiration about aging and the second half of life than ever before. There are also more fabulous role models—beautiful and vibrant people who are leading rich, full lives in their fifties, sixties, seventies, and beyond. These men and women are creating a new paradigm for a fierce elder, a juicy crone: Gloria Steinem, Helen Mirren, Diana Nyad, Edie Windsor, Mary Oliver, Ram Dass, Billy Crystal, Louise Hay, Jean Shinoda Bolen, Michael Meade, Pema Chödrön, David Whyte.

No doubt you have many examples from your own family and friends or favorite historical figures—Georgia O'Keeffe, Carl Jung, the poet May Sarton, to name a few. Celebrate, honor, and emulate them. Consider creating a vision board with their photographs and quotations. Begin bringing their energy and inspiration into your life. One of the greatest things we can aspire to as we age is to become a role model for the younger generations.

The Secret of the Second Saturn Return

As our involvement in the world begins to wind down (again, the key word here is *begins*) around age fifty-eight, the roles we've had while creating a personal and professional identity, raising a family, etc., naturally shift. The new purpose and fresh sources of energy that will support us in the years ahead won't come from the outer world. That is why the inner work is so essential. It is through the soul work that we develop the depth, wisdom, and compassion that are the foundation for this new phase.

*Throughout our lives, transitions require that we ask for help
and allow ourselves to yield to forces stronger than our wills or our
egos' desires. As transitions take place during our later years, a
fundamental and primal shift from ambition to meaning occurs.*
—Angeles Arrien, *The Second Half of Life*

No doubt, many of you have big jobs, a presence in the world (and on Twitter and Facebook), and no plans to retire. In fact, for many people, it all comes together in this third act. Nevertheless, some fine tuning is necessary. Arianna Huffington is a good example. A super A-type personality who cofounded the *Huffington Post* in 2005, she typically worked eighteen-hour days. In 2007, she fell asleep at her desk and woke up on the floor, lying in a pool of blood, having cut her eye and broken her cheekbone on the corner of her desk when she collapsed. She was fifty-seven years old at the time.

After extensive medical tests, her doctors found nothing wrong besides extreme exhaustion and lack of sleep. "This was the classic wake-up call," she writes in her book, *Thrive*. "Looking back on my life, I had other times when I should have woken up but didn't. This time I really did and made many changes in the way I live my life, including adopting daily practices to keep me on track—and out of doctors' waiting rooms."[21]

Her book is the result of what she learned and how she came to redefine success to include well-being, wisdom, compassion, and giving. These days, the *Huffington Post* offices have naps rooms, a gym, plus meditation and yoga classes.

---

[21]Arianna Huffington, *Thrive: The Third Metric to Redefining Success and Creating a Life of Well-Being, Wisdom and Wonder* (New York: Harmony Books, 2014), p. 2.

What Doesn't Work: We've all seen people who are trapped in an earlier period of their life; a time when they had money, power, or great beauty. But the world has moved on, and they've remained in a time warp. If we don't make the transition and find something that brings us alive and inspires us, then we remain stuck in an old persona and are vulnerable to becoming "the old fool" rather than the "wise elder."

"Eldering for me is a process word," writes Rabbi Zalman, "a verb that connotes change and movement. It doesn't connote the unchanging frozen state of a noun." Engage. Engage. Engage.

What Works: Saturn is Father Time, and we can't hold him back. Part of the Saturn process is making peace with ourselves, our past, and the whole process of aging. It takes years, but this cycle is our initiation. There's something very beautiful and inspiring about someone who is at ease with themselves and their age. "Bien dans sa peau," is a well-known French phrase meaning "comfortable in your skin."

The opposite of old is not young. The opposite of old is new. As long as we continue to experience the new, we will gloriously inhabit all of the ages that we are.
—SARK

Rituals: Public ceremonies and rituals help us close the door to the past and reinforce our commitment and our readiness to embrace a new phase. In his book, Rabbi Zalman explains how people in Japan mark their sixtieth birthday with a celebration that includes wearing special red garments that proclaim their new elder status and freedom from social obligations. "Elder initiation rites formally sever our ties to midlife goals and aspirations, replacing them with the freedom and wider concerns of elderhood."

Jean Haner, author of *The Wisdom of Your Face* and other books, has this to say: "In Chinese culture, turning 60 is the single most important birthday of your life, considered to be the completion of one full life cycle, when you are now freed of old responsibilities and can move forward in a new way!"

Ritual: Kate converted to Judaism in her mid-forties, having attended services with her Jewish husband for more than fifteen years. It was a meaningful life choice she came to on her own. As her thirteenth year as a Jew approached, around the time of her fifty-ninth birthday, she decided she wanted to read from the Torah—like most thirteen-year-olds at bar and bat mitzvahs. Rather than simply memorizing the portion she had been assigned, she wanted to stand before that scroll having gained the ability to read it, which she did during the ceremony in front of her family, friends, and community. Her actions brought her to the status of "adult" as her Jewish self, while simultaneously becoming a true elder. Meanwhile, unlike actual thirteen-year-olds, she planned her own party afterward.

Saturn Wisdom: Carolyn G. Heilbrun notes, "What they never tell you about age, some pundit once observed, is that it's such a delightful change from being young. The secret is to view the passing of youth as gain, not loss."

My Second Saturn Return

The period between when I sold my restaurant in New York City (at fifty-two) until my Second Saturn Return (at fifty-eight) can best be described as fumbling, floundering, and trying to figure it out. I was doing a little of everything.

My passion for astrology continued to grow as I took classes and attended lectures and conferences. I even began doing some readings, but not enough to support myself; at that point, I wasn't thinking of astrology as a career. I patched together a living doing a series of part-time jobs; at various times I worked as a salesperson in a Native American jewelry store, as an assistant in a public relations firm, teaching computers at Methadone clinics, even dog walking. These jobs supported me while I focused on writing a book with my good friend Lyn Skreczko. It was entitled *The Manhattan Health Pages: A Resource Guide to Educate, Pamper, and Inspire You;* it was published in late 1999.

The Manhattan Health Pages was a guide to everything healthy and holistic in New York City. The book was published by a small but classy local publisher, and although the book turned out beautifully, it didn't sell well. I had envisioned it as akin to a *Zagat Guide* to health in New York City, but it needed a couple more years to gain momentum.

In retrospect, the book was an extension of my old life in the world of health foods—a world that was over, only I didn't realize it. This project turned out to be a *long* detour (the story of my life), but it eventually brought me back to astrology.

My plan was to use my background in the natural food industry, combined with the book, to create a new career writing and lecturing on health and wellness. Makes sense, right? It seemed to work in the beginning. Lyn and I did a lot of TV interviews and lectured at corporations like Viacom and Comedy Central. Then the corporate lectures on urban health led to lectures on astrology. An editor I approached about doing some freelance writing on spas offered me a chance to write a Sun sign column; that column led to others.

Around 1999, Steven Forrest began his apprenticeship program in California. I found out about it in 2000 and signed up, flying to Southern California twice a year. Not only is Steven a master astrologer, but he's also a brilliant communicator and a wise and compassionate person. The seminars at Blue Sky Ranch, outside San Diego, were exciting, inspiring, and exactly what I needed.

Evolutionary Astrology isn't just another astrological technique; it's based on the values of freedom, responsibility, and respect for people's innate ability to grow and change. I resonated with Steven's approach, and that became the basis for my own astrological work.

Meanwhile, I was under enormous financial pressure. I was really winging it the last couple of years the restaurant was open, at times using credit cards to cover bills. That led me to refinance my house in East Hampton, which gave me a bigger mortgage. Plus, I was still paying off the restaurant in Great Barrington! I continued juggling a couple of part-time jobs during this period, and although it wasn't easy, things slowly began to fall into place.

Someone I worked for was instrumental in helping me land some Sun sign columns. Even the dog walking job led to a gig writing an astrology column for *TV Guide*! There's a saying, "Ride the horse in the direction its going." I finally decided to do just that. My Second Saturn Return had its challenges, but it was also a rich time of learning, growing, and, most of all, laying the foundation for my third act.

Stories
Dominick Dunne

Dunne was once a big Hollywood producer, but he lost his marriage, career, and reputation as a result of alcohol and drugs; he became a pariah and a laughing stock. He was so broke, he sold everything he had, including his dog (which says it all), and drove to Oregon, where he lived in a tiny cabin. There he wrote a book entitled *Winners;* it didn't do very well, but it was a start. Unfortunately, it would get worse before it got better.

His daughter, Dominque Dunne, was murdered by her former boyfriend. Shortly before the trial began, Dominick ran into editor Tina Brown, who was about to take over *Vanity Fair;* she suggested he take notes during the trial, so he did. The result was an article he wrote for *Vanity Fair* entitled, "Justice: A Father's Account of the Trial of his Daughter's Killer." That article led to a contract with the magazine, a brilliant new career, and a passion for justice. He was fifty-eight years old.

Shirley's Story

Shirley Soffer's interest in astrology didn't begin until she was in her early fifties. At the time, she was working in publishing; during her lunch hour, she found herself drawn to a nearby bookstore that carried astrology books. She began reading them and never stopped. She started studying astrology seriously a few years later.

By the time of her Second Saturn Return, Shirley had become certified by the NCGR (National Council for Geocosmic Research)—a national astrology organization—and was building her practice; eventually, she started lecturing and publishing articles. She also created her popular Wednesday night class that, twenty-five years later, is still going strong. In 1998, when she was sixty-four, she wrote her book, *The Astrology Sourcebook.*

"I had been in a marriage, raised a family, and worked in different fields, but I didn't have any one area that was mine. Astrology was the missing piece of the puzzle. Once I had that, it all came together;

my beliefs, my interest in mythology, dreams, art, literature, and religion. Most important, I had life experience, the emotional depth and the maturity." At eighty-two, Shirley is still doing what she loves. "Every day is a blessing. I'm grateful to be alive," she says.

Sting

In 2009, the singer Sting released an album entitled *If on a Winter's Night*. Deeper, darker, more spiritual and contemplative than his previous music, this album seems like a meditation on winter, the Christmas season, and perhaps aging as well. Saturn is sometimes referred to as the lord of winter, and at our Second Saturn Return, we enter the winter of our life. Sting was fifty-eight at the time and going through his own Second Saturn Return.

THE CLOSING URANUS SQUARE
A Second Wind (Ages 62–63)

The years beyond sixty, the years of our second maturity,
may be evolution's greatest gift to humanity.
—Jean Houston

There is a colorful, energizing—and even a bit feisty—aspect that follows the Saturn Return. This is the closing Uranus square, and it takes place between the ages of sixty-two and sixty-three when that maverick Uranus is in its home stretch. By now, it has traveled three quarters of the way from where it began, and this is the last aspect it makes before returning to the position it occupied at birth. That is called the Uranus Return, and it takes place around age eighty-four.

By that time, Uranus will have contacted every other planet in the birth chart, and ideally (as Carl Jung might say) we become fully individualized—provided that we've been living *authentically*. If we haven't been living authentically, then the closing Uranus square in our early sixties gives us a chance to correct that.

How? Remember, change-at-all-costs Uranus is the chief architect of our Midlife Journey at age forty-two, when it is exactly opposite its natal position. It's the planet of freedom and rebellion, so we've got to break some rules, make some trouble, and take some chances. I'm not talking about rebelling for the sake of rebelling, but if there is something you want to do, be, or have, then now's the time to act on it.

Who do you want to be at eighty-four? Hopefully someone well marinated from a full, rich, and juicy life; someone who is wise, compassionate, and spirited; the kind of person who can look back at his or her life with considerable satisfaction and minimal regret. The decisions we make in our early sixties will influence what the kind of older person we become in our eighties.

How's that for incentive? Think of Georgia O'Keeffe, fashion icon Diana Vreeland, activist Maggie Kuhn, Carl Jung, James Hillman, or Joseph Campbell in their eighties. These great role models lived fully right up to the end of their lives; they didn't put on the breaks in their sixties, they accelerated!

The Showgirl Must Go On!
—Bette Midler

In June 2008, Bette Midler appeared on *Oprah* to talk about her new show, *The Showgirl Must Go On,* that was about to open in Las Vegas. The Divine Miss M committed to performing five nights a week for the next two years; ambitious for any age, let alone at sixty-two! In the beginning, she alternated with Cher (also sixty-two). Bette, Cher, and this fabulous show serves as a great metaphor for the closing Uranus square. Not everyone at sixty-two has the stamina or talent to sing and dance like a showgirl, but we can all invent or reinvent our own third act and perform it with all the spunk and bravado of a star!

We even get a boost between sixty and sixty-one, thanks to a fifth Jupiter Return followed by the grand sextile. The grand sextile is a mathematical technique that involves moving all the planets sixty degrees (one degree for each year), which creates a sextile (a harmonious aspect), giving us "some wind beneath our wings." These two optimistic aspects bestow a blessing for this new decade making it the perfect launching pad for the Uranus square.

* Diana Nyad swam from Cuba to Florida at age sixty-four.

* Jane Fonda left Ted Turner in her early sixties and started a brand-new life.

* At age sixty, Madeleine Albright became the first woman to head the State Department.

* Patti Smith published her first book, *Just Kids*.

What kind of elders do you imagine they will be at eighty-four? And what about Bette Midler, Meryl Streep, Dr. Christiane Northrup (author of *Goddesses Never Age*), and Billy Crystal? I see them as gutsy, fearless, still creating, still living fully.

What Do You Plan to Do in Your Wild and Precious Elder Years?

"Tell me, what do you plan to do with your one wild and precious life?" Mary Oliver's beautiful line from her beloved poem, "A Summer's Day," has inspired countless people. We think of people asking that question at the beginning of their life, but, in fact, we can ask it at any time and at any age.

Who do you want to be in your older years? What kind of life do you want to be living? How do you want to feel? And, perhaps most important of all, what kind of attitude do you need? What actions can you take *now* that will help create that future? What habits, thoughts, and attachments do you need to let go of?

> *The old woman I shall become will be quite different from*
> *the woman I am now. Another I is beginning.*
> —George Sand

In her workshops, webinars, and books, author and artist Susan Ariel Rainbow Kennedy (aka SARK) suggests writing a letter to yourself from your Inner Wise Self as a way to quiet the Inner Critics (those "mean girls" and thugs we carry around in our heads, who torment and intimidate us). I love the idea of an Inner Wise Elder, who is really an aspect of our Wise Self.

Why not write a letter to yourself from your Inner Wise Elder? Make it lavish and positive; be extravagant, and do it often. It's a wonderful way to establish a relationship with your future self.

When I picture my own Inner Wise Elder, I envision her ensconced in the tower of the Astrology Café that I write about in my newsletters. Dressed in her purple velvet cloak and surrounded by her sacred statues, she sits at her round oak table with her runes, stones, and cards spread out before her, dispensing wisdom and compassion. I often ask her for advice, and I always receive it.

Beloved Daughter,

Know that you are seen, you are safe, you are supported, and you are loved. Let go of all the shoulds and musts, the litany of outer rituals and routines. Trust your heart; listen to the goddess within; listen loudly. Slow down. Breathe. Be still. It is from this tender place, this place of allowing and expansion that you need to live as well as write. Stay away from the urban madness in your mind; the heavy traffic, the crowds and voices. Step into the lush garden of your heart, with its gentle streams and scented flowers—lilacs, roses, peonies. Rest in the small sacred arbors, for it is in this rich and generous solitude that everything flourishes, prospers, and grows. All is well; you are loved.

Wabi-Sabi

I love the Japanese term *wabi-sabi*, which, by the way, is not a garnish for sushi. Wabi-sabi describes an aesthetic based on imperfection, irregularity, simplicity, economy, modesty, and intimacy.

* *Wabi* is associated with rustic simplicity, quietness, and an understated elegance in nature as well as in manmade objects.

* *Sabi* refers to the beauty or serenity that comes with age.

The most common examples of wabi-sabi include a bowl, a tea cup, wood, paper, or fabric. Imagine a bowl whose patina has been worn off; one that contains some cracks and chips but is well used and loved and has with the passage of time become more interesting. Could a person be wabi-sabi?

Several years ago, I had some therapy with a Jungian analyst; a lovely woman who I guessed to be in her mid- to late sixties. I was discussing her with a friend who also knew her; although I could talk about my sessions with the therapist, I found it difficult to describe her physically. My friend said it was probably because she had let go of a lot of ego. That made perfect sense to me.

When I think of wabi-sabi in relation to a person, I imagine someone who has shed a great deal of their ego and has let go of the need to prove themselves. It's as if the outer veneer of personality has softened and become more porous, so that their essence, their soul, shines through. Gloria Steinem is a great example; so are Pema Chödrön, Mary Oliver, Thich Nhat Hanh, and Ram Dass. I want to age like that, perhaps less polished on the surface but hopefully more real, more genuine; fully present, at ease with myself and the world.

The Bucket List

The Bucket List is a great ritual and the perfect metaphor for this period. When Uranus is in our lives, we're feeling restless, frisky, adventurous, and more inclined to push the envelope. This is not about doing something that doesn't feel right, but we don't learn anything by never venturing outside our comfort zone.

If you've never thought about sky diving and the idea makes you sick to your stomach, it's probably not for you. But if you've always secretly dreamed of going white water rafting down the Colorado River or learning to tango, maybe even in Argentina, but simply never got around to it, then perhaps that's something you should consider. You know it is right if, in spite of your fear, you feel really excited about doing it.

What's on your Bucket List? What have you always wanted to do but never allowed yourself to try, or never before had the opportunity to try? It doesn't have to be dangerous or cost a lot of money; it just has to be something that inspires and energizes you. Maybe it's researching your ancestors, getting a tattoo, self-publishing a book of your poems or stories, or finally learning to meditate.

What about taking a course on how to design a website, reading *War and Peace* or *The Lord of the Rings,* being photographed nude, or learning to speak Japanese? With hundreds of websites devoted to Bucket Lists, there's no end to the rousing ideas or possible adventures. And although a Bucket List experience may be temporary, it gets the energy moving in the right direction and builds momentum. Besides, you never know where it will lead. Just like a casual date can turn into a love affair or marriage, a Bucket List jaunt may transform into a late-in-life passion or career.

I never thought in terms of my own Bucket List; I'm grateful to be doing astrology readings and writing at this point in my life. But lately, an old idea has been nudging me. I would love to go to college and get a degree! In the late sixties and early seventies, I took lots of classes at New York University and the New School for Social Research (mainly film and writing), but, being somewhat of a hippie, I never considered getting credit for any of them.

At the same time, I was participating in tons of self-help programs, spiritual disciplines, and retreats; and since the early nineties, I've been studying astrology. But I want to study psychology and literature in a more formal way. It turns out that many colleges, such as Hunter College in New York City and Smith College in Massachusetts, offer free tuition for seniors, and I can go at my own pace. Sure, I'll be in my late seventies, maybe even eighty when I graduate, but so what? I'm going to be that age anyway.

Road Scholar

Road Scholar (originally called Elderhostel) was founded by two friends in 1975; Marty Knowles, a free-spirited hippie, and David

Bianco, a university administer. They joined forces to create this unique not-for-profit organization that provides educational adventures and learning experiences to adults over fifty.

It offers over five thousand tours in America, Canada, and 150 other countries. It's an exciting and economical way to travel, learn, and make lifelong friends. They even offer intergenerational learning adventures, so you can invite the grandkids.

Road Scholar is known for its great instructors and interesting programs. They even have scholarships for courses in North America. An exciting new program called Living and Learning allows you to live abroad in one city for four to six weeks and immerse yourself in the language and culture. Who hasn't dreamed of living in Paris, Florence, or Barcelona? What a perfect way to make that happen. I haven't been to Europe in years, but this has me dreaming about returning to Rome. It seems my Bucket List is getting longer!

The Moral Bucket List

New York Times op-ed writer David Brooks didn't set out to travel cross-country on a motorcycle or climb Mount Everest; instead, he went on an extensive inner journey. Inspired by people who he describes as "deeply good," he set out to discover how those folks got that way.

The result was his bestselling book, *The Road to Character.* His focus was not on outer achievement and ambitions but on inner values.

> In this method, you don't ask, What do I want from life? You ask a different set of questions: What does life want from me? What are my circumstances calling me to do?

In this scheme of things, we don't create our lives; we are summoned by life.[22]

You're 65 and You Can't Hide!

Throughout my life, there has always been a number that sounded old. When I was 16, it was 27; at 29, it was 42; at 38, it was 52. At 65, however, it was 65.
—Mark Jacobson, *New York* magazine (April 2014)

There are certain ages that seem to carry more weight, and sixty-five is definitely one of them. We can color our hair, run marathons, and eat lots of kale, but at sixty-five, we can no longer ignore the elephant (or rather the *senior*) in the room. We may not feel or even look old, but let's face it, there's a stigma attached to sixty-five; it's *serious.*

These days, people are living and working longer, but since 1935 (the year the Social Security Act was passed), sixty-five has been the official age at which one retires. It's a marker; the great dividing line. Medicare kicks in, and somehow that seals the deal. It's not just our age that changes, but our place in society does as well, and it's not unusual to feel like an outsider; no longer relevant, no longer at the center of the action. And once we cross that mountain, it's an express train to seventy and onward toward *old age.* No matter how positive or perky you are, we all think of these things at some point. I know I do.

The Reality of Aging: The Second Stage of Eldering

At fifty-eight, our Second Saturn Return is the first stage of becoming an elder; but we're just entering that phase—we're an apprentice elder. The Saturn Return is a conjunction that has a quality

---

[22]David Brooks, *The Road to Character* (New York: Random House, 2015), p. 21.

of newness and naïveté. The second phase of eldering takes place between sixty-five and sixty-six, when transiting Saturn makes a demanding square to its natal position.

As you know by now, no-frills Saturn is that planet of reality; cold, hard, and sobering. It's not unusual to suddenly wake up as if from a dream and realize that the posse is probably not going to show up; neither is the prince (or princess). I'm an optimistic person; I believe we can change and grow at any age, but if we've been drifting, Saturn can be a wake-up call. Social Security begins at age sixty-six; some people may choose to start earlier or later, but sixty-six is the age when we receive full benefits. That's a good metaphor for Saturn. We're receiving support, according to what we've put in—and, in true Saturn fashion, nothing more.

At sixty-five, we're confronted with some weighty decisions. Should I retire or not? Can I even afford to? And when? It's not unusual for people in their sixties to still have parents that they're responsible for; either living at home or in a nursing facility. We have to navigate Medicare, deal with finances, family, and the future. These are daunting issues, Saturn issues. Uncharted territory.

The last ten years in the US have been dramatic. The economy crashed in 2008 along with the collapse of many financial institutions, followed by massive layoffs. In 2012, the East Coast was hit by Hurricane Sandy. Many people lost their pensions and their homes; retirement was suddenly no longer an option. We can see folks who lost their jobs in the corporate world working now at Whole Foods or Trader Joe's. I know a number of people who confronted their financial situation in their mid-sixties; they declared bankruptcy, started over, and rebuilt their credit. Saturn's aspect in our mid-sixties can serve to get us back on track.

Not retire, re-fire!
—Michael Meade, *Finding Genius in Your Life* (CD)

Even if we can afford to retire, it's not unusual to find ourselves in a rut once we finally do. We're used to having a full schedule, a career, and a place to go to, and suddenly there's a void; it can feel like falling into an abyss. We can lose a physical structure, as well as our professional identity. Although it's not a prediction, many people are vulnerable to depression at this point, and depression is associated with the ringed planet.

Marv's Story

Marv had been one of my very first employees when I opened my restaurant in 1974. He started off as a dishwasher, then became a waiter. One summer, he managed the restaurant for me so I could do a residential workshop in Vermont. It had been thirty-five years since I last heard from him, so it was a real surprise when he emailed me recently. He was in town for a seminar, and he wanted to get together.

We met for tea at a Starbucks in Chelsea and spent two wonderful hours taking nonstop. I was surprised to learn that he had been working in the corporate world. In our restaurant days, he had been studying tai chi, meditating, and going to consciousness seminars. He told me he had retired recently, when he was sixty-eight. His company had offered him a generous exit package, and it had taken him thirty seconds to decide.

With nothing to do, he ended up watching television for several hours a day and fell into a depression. As a result, he began taking antianxiety medication. Luckily, he was also reading a great deal and stumbled on a self-help book, *The Inside Out Revolution*. He became so psyched about it that he was able to get off his meds and started taking workshops with the author. He didn't know where it would lead, but he felt excited about life; he was learning, growing, and meeting terrific people. I wouldn't be surprised if he ended up teaching the material.

Everything I've ever let go of has claw marks on it.
—David Foster Wallace

During a Saturn transit, old structures often collapse, familiar reference points disappear, and we're encouraged to create new ones. The more we cling to an old role or identity, the harder it will be to make the shift. Saturn is not asking us to let go of what is working; it's asking us to release what's not supporting us and to rebuild our foundation. It's important to remember that it's an inside job and not merely an outer goal. Just as at the Saturn Return, a life review, therapy, and support groups can be valuable tools. Doing creative work can help unlock emotions and get the juices flowing. Some people end up taking medication—and sometimes that's necessary in the short term—but it isn't a replacement for dealing with the deeper issues.

If you fall into a rut, don't furnish it.
—author unknown

How do you get out of a rut? Years ago, my friend Roger was attending a spiritual gathering. A revered guru from India was seated onstage, answering questions from the audience. After every question, which included the whole gamut—health, sex, love, death, money, etc.—the guru would exclaim, "Achep, achep!"

Roger couldn't understand what the guru was saying and thought perhaps he had a cold and was sneezing. Finally, out of frustration, he turned to the woman next to him and asked what the guru was saying. "Accept!" the woman replied. That kind of sums it up—about life *and* aging. We can't control everything that happens to us, but we can control how we respond. Accepting a situation is the first step to changing it.

What Saturn is asking us to do at this stage is to accept the limitations of aging, but that doesn't mean we have to be defined by them. In fact, once we accept something and stop fighting against it, it has the chance to soften and ultimately shift. It takes time to establish new a role, a new dimension of identity, and we need to be gentle with ourselves. It's important not to label or demonize the situation or ourselves. Allow it to be there, but also open up to what else is there. What are you grateful for, what's good in your life, what brings you alive?

As Pema Chodron writes in *When Things Fall Apart,* "Sticking with that uncertainty, getting the knack of relaxing in the midst of chaos, learning not to panic—this is the spiritual path."

No one has taught us more about the spiritual path than the much-loved teacher, Ram Dass. Now he is teaching us about aging and the end of life. In his book *Still Here: Embracing Aging, Changing, and Dying,* Ram Dass describes riding the train from Connecticut to New York one autumn evening after a day of hiking with a friend. The conductor approached and asked him what kind of ticket he wanted. He hadn't realized he had a choice.

"Regular or senior citizen," the conductor explained. Ram Dass wrote that although he was then sixty-two, bald, with age spots and gout, it had never occurred to him that he could be considered a senior citizen. This revelation got him thinking deeply about aging, and he decided to apply his thirty-five years of spiritual work to learning about this new phase of life.

At sixty-six, Ram Dass suffered a near-fatal stroke that left him paralyzed on the right side. In his book and in the movie about his life, *Fierce Grace,* he speaks about "being stroked." Being highly independent, it wasn't easy for him to receive help, but he turned his illness into a spiritual lesson. "Before my stroke, I would never have dreamed I could be as peaceful as I am with the attention of other people, or that I could allow people to 'invade my privacy' to the degree that I have, but these experiences have touched me very deeply."[23]

Sixty and Me

Margaret Manning is a writer, entrepreneur, digital nomad, and founder of Sixty and Me, an online community, newsletter, and website for woman over sixty. I love the passion and enthusiasm Margaret has for her work, and I have followed Sixty and Me religiously for years. It reaches a global community of over 250,000 women, and her weekly newsletter goes out to over 30,000 women. She has a following of over 75,000 women on Facebook and writes for *Huffington Post.*

Margaret has created thousands of articles and videos on every imaginable subject—from sex and dating to death and dying. She has interviewed experts and written on topics ranging from health, fashion, beauty, retirement, travel, and reinvention. It's an incredible resource.

Margaret was born in London but has lived all over the world. She worked as a marketing and communications manager for

---

[23]Ram Dass, *Still Here: Embracing Aging, Changing, and Dying* (New York: Riverhead Books, 2000), p. 95.

Microsoft before packing it in and launching Sixty and Me. She also organized a TEDx event in London in 2013. Margaret is a great example of someone who has not only reinvented herself in the second half of life but is helping others to do it.

Happiness Peaks at Age 65!

According to Sonja Lyubomirsky, a professor in the Department of Psychology at the University of California and author of *The How of Happiness,* happiness actually peaks at age sixty-five! In her book, she describes a twenty-two-year study that was done with about two thousand healthy veterans of World War II and the Korean War, which revealed that life satisfaction actually increased over the course of these men's lives, peaked at age sixty-five, and didn't start significantly declining until age seventy-five.

Other studies corroborate this. A recent survey, spearheaded by the Office of National Statistics in Britain, involved 300,000 adults over a three-year period; it revealed that people between forty-five and fifty-nine had the lowest satisfaction with their lives, but those sixty-five and beyond scored highest in all-round contentment.

Another survey was commissioned by tech giant Samsung involving two thousand Brits. They found that at age thirty-five, people were the least happy—which makes sense when you think of the responsibilities of balancing career, relationships, and parenting. The survey discovered that fifty-eight is the age at which people are the most content. So if you're not happy at thirty or forty or fifty, don't give up; there's still time!

The fifties are great, but the sixties can be even more freeing. Gene D. Cohen (in his book *The Creative Age*) describes this period as the Liberation Phase.

If we look beyond age markers and search instead for the underlying development phase of adult life, we find that it is defined by a kind of personal liberation combined with life experience that lifts inhibitions and gives the courage to ignore social conventions that restrict our creative expression.[24]

"Only after sixty my true life began." At age sixty, Bodhi Hanna Kistner quit her job and moved from Germany to India. Then she started practicing Kyudo, Japanese Zen archery. At seventy, she began teaching Kyudo. Now she's eighty-six, and she gives lessons in India, California, and Hawaii.[25]

From Drinking Lattes to Serving Them Up

Working at Starbucks wasn't exactly on Michael Gill's Bucket List but, like one of those Outward Bound adventures, it turned out to be exactly what he needed. Broke, desperate, out of work, no medical insurance, and in poor health (he was diagnosed with a brain tumor), at age sixty-three, Michael Gill took a job in Starbucks and finally grew up. It's funny how life conspires to put us in touch with our destiny.

Michael was raised on the Upper East Side, went to Yale University, and upon graduation, entered the advertising business. He lived in a big house in the suburbs, had a six-figure income, and enjoyed power lunches and all the trappings of a successful business man. Then, after twenty-six years as a creative director at the

[24]Gene D. Cohen, *The Creative Age: Awakening Human Potential in the Second Half of Life* (New York: HarperCollins, 2000), p. 84.
[25]Interview with Bodhi Hanna Kistner, *http://theageofhappiness.com.*

J. Walter Thompson advertising agency, he was fired. He was fifty-five years old. For a few years, he tried to survive by being a consultant, but eventually he ran out of clients, money, and hope.

One day while sitting in Starbucks (which had basically become his office), feeling miserable and scared, a young woman approached him and asked if he would like a job there. Unbeknownst to him, there was a hiring event going on. Stunned, he said "yes," filled out an application, and ended up taking the job.

By his own admission, he was arrogant, prejudiced, and an elitist. He took a big risk, but that risk was fueled by his willingness to finally accept his situation and do something about it. At Starbucks, Michael learned to make lattes, clean toilets, and work with young people a third his age. More important, he humbled up, made peace with his own children, and found dignity, health insurance, and happiness. Starbucks not only saved his life, it saved his soul.

The Politics of Aging

As you can see, I'm just beginning to realize the upcoming pleasures of being a nothing-to-lose, take-no-shit older woman; of looking at what once seemed outer limits as just road signs.
—Gloria Steinem, "Doing Sixty," *Moving Beyond Words*

On her fortieth birthday, Gloria Steinem became an instant spokesperson on age discrimination when a reporter's casual comment on her youthful looks elicited her famous comeback, "This is what forty looks like. We've been lying so long, who would know?"

That was in 1974, and the pressure for women to lie about their age (plus the lengths they would go to hide it) was enormous—which is why she chose to celebrate her birthday publicly and continues to do so every year. Her comment caused an overwhelming response back then and exposed the taboo women face from age stereotyping; it also opened up a conversation that's been going on ever since.

In "Doing Sixty," the powerful and inspiring essay from her book *Moving Beyond Words,* Steinem discusses this issue, as well as her own aging process, the unexpected freedom she discovered, and the crucial events and people that helped shape her life. This thirty-seven-page essay is filled with great insights and reflections, as well as many of her famous quotes. I cannot recommend it enough.

In her essay, Steinem writes that she doesn't feel calmer and more serene as she ages; rather, she feels more intensely. She emphasizes the importance of change. "Clinging to the past is the problem. Embracing change is the solution." But she also acknowledges the need she felt in her fifties to develop her inner life and create more self-care. "It's taken me a long time to realize that when I said so defiantly at fifty, 'I'm going to go right on doing everything I did at thirty and forty,' this wasn't progress. I was refusing to change and thus robbing myself of the future."

We all need to change and grow but not in a militant way and not at the expense of who we are. The change needs to come from an inner need and not an outer pressure. Perhaps it all comes down to being authentic (a word often associated with the planet Uranus); going at our own speed, honoring our boundaries, and not letting the outside world dictate our choices.

Transitions

One of my favorite books is *The Way of Transition: Embracing Life's Most Difficult Moments,* by William Bridges. I wrote about his book in the chapter called the Midlife Journey, because what he says about transition is so valuable in dealing with any kind of crises or change, including these generational cycles. Now, here is William Bridge's own story.

Bridges was an author (*Transitions: Making Sense of Life's Changes; Job Shift: How to Prosper in a Workplace without Jobs;* etc.) and a consultant on transition for various organizations. Don't you love the fact that his name is Bridges and his specialty is transitions?

When he was in his early sixties, his wife of thirty-seven years died; although he was an expert on the subject of transition, he wasn't prepared for the unknown and uncomfortable place where he found himself. He suddenly felt as if he didn't know a thing about this business of transition.

Being around people was difficult; so was working. To his credit, he hung out in that in-between place and mined it for all it was worth. He spent time alone, he traveled, but mostly he thought deeply and consciously about his life, his marriage, and the choices he had made. In a sense, he did his own version of a life review.

What he discovered made him rethink the whole subject of transitions and to open his heart in a way that had been impossible before. This led him to write the book *The Way of Transition.* Unlike his other books, this one is deeply personal and intimate; he shares honestly and openly about his own struggles, the challenges in his marriage, his wife's illness, and his own journey. That is why I resonate with it; I learn best from knowing people's stories and finding out how they transformed.

Around the same time, Bridges met and fell in love with the woman who would become his second wife. His story is an inspiring example of what's possible when we're willing to do the inner exploratory work and how that exploration can lead to change in our outer world.

My Own Uranus Square Uranus

By age sixty, I was doing astrology readings and writing Sun sign columns for a few small magazines, but it still wasn't enough to pay the hefty mortgage on my house on Long Island. After I closed my restaurant, I had refinanced the house (again), so the mortgage was high and it was a constant source of stress. I was still juggling a couple of part-time jobs, and I felt like a gerbil on a treadmill; I could never get to what I really wanted to do—my own writing.

I loved my house near Acobonic Bay in the Springs section of East Hampton; it was such a healing place, a true sanctuary. Being a double Taurus, nature is vital for my soul, and the house and the land with its mature trees plus the nearby bay were essential to my well-being. Over the years, I had often toyed with the idea of selling it, but I always backed down; it meant too much to me. I rented it out during the summer, which was a huge help with the mortgage, but that last summer, I had trouble renting it, and that threw me into a panic. I finally realized I simply couldn't live with the constant stress; I had to get off the treadmill. I knew my Uranus square Uranus was approaching and realized it was time to take a big risk.

At the same time, I was having a Pluto transit; Pluto was opposite my Venus, which can often bring a loss of a love or of something you love. It wasn't my first waltz with Pluto, so I knew it meant I needed to look at the deeper meaning, face my own dark side, and heal an old wound. Selling my house was one of the most painful things I ever did; I felt as if I was losing a beloved friend. But it made me examine how I've treated the things I've loved and lost; the restaurant, money, and now the house. After I sold it I did some therapy, with the aforementioned Jungian analyst, that was deeply healing for me.

As heartbreaking as selling the house was, it was also liberating. Several months after I sold it, I gave up the last of my part-time jobs. I was totally free—for the first time in years! This was the final piece. I was able to pay off credit cards, loans, not to mention my second restaurant in Great Barrington. I still think about the house with great tenderness and miss my sacred haven, but I understand now that selling it provided me with another kind of haven; one in which to write, do astrology, and build a new life, and for this I am profoundly grateful.

My sixties were a time when my life really came together, and I finally felt "all of one piece." What I was doing in the world was finally consistent with who I was inside. I actually felt content, even happy, for the first time in my life. I'd never been a truly happy person. I wouldn't say I was sad, only rather steadily melancholy. But I began to feel truly happy. Who knew such a thing was possible and at this age?

The Uranus Process: We're not all Gloria Steinem, Bette Midler, or Diana Nyad, but we can learn from them. Even taking into consideration our own abilities and limitations, there are still areas in which we can stretch and grow. Taking risks, even small ones, exploring new areas, and forming new habits will not only empower our sixties, it will shape who we become at eighty-four, when Uranus comes full circle.

If we've done the work in the Second Saturn Return, finding a new role, a fresh purpose, then the Uranus period in our early sixties gives us the freedom to jazz it up a bit. You built the house, now you decorate it! If you haven't found that purpose, it's not too late. In fact, this is the ideal time. What all those women have in common is that they had an objective. We don't have to do what they did, but we do need to find something that is aligned with who we are. As activist Maggie Kuhn said, "There must be a goal at every stage of life! There must be a goal!"

The Saturn Process: Every seven years, Saturn comes around, and, in a sense, we're back to square one; time again to face reality, take a personal inventory, and deal with the new issues and responsibilities that the Saturn phase brings. Sometimes it "takes a village"— be willing to ask for advice and support. For many of us, that can be the biggest hurdle.

Saturn represents structure; even if you're not working, you still need to create a routine and make new habits to support your current life. The good news? Saturn isn't given to one night stands and casual flings; new routines and behaviors created during a Saturn period have an excellent chance of enduring. This is why the Uranus phase in our early sixties is so important; taking risks, discovering new interests, and learning new skills creates the necessary momentum and confidence to deal with the Saturn period.

What Doesn't Work: Staying stuck in the past and the way things used to be, then complaining about it. As author Caroline Myss says, "Complaining, blaming is so last century." Plus, it's not healthy; not for your immune system or your cells. Become an elder, *not an older.*

What Works: Healthy elders are future oriented; they live in the present and the future. They have goals, plans. They are risk takers and rebels; they don't belong to the herd. Find something that you love to do and get involved, engaged. Stay curious, continue to learn and grow. Move your body; open your mind. Seek out great role models; better yet, become one!

Uranus Wisdom: "Age has given me what I was looking for my entire life—it has given me *me*. It provided the time and the experience and failures and triumphs and friends who helped me step into the shape that had been waiting for me all my life. . . . I not only get along with me most of the time now, I am militantly and maternally on my own side." (Anne Lamott)

Rituals: "My husband gave me the Taj Mahal for my sixty-fifth birthday!" Kate had always wanted to visit India, but since it wasn't someplace that also interested her husband, she never went. Last year, a friend found a luxurious tour and encouraged Kate to join her. "I decided to give my husband the gift of giving me something I truly, truly wanted," Kate said. "He gave it to me with a generosity of resources and spirit that I will remember along with the adventure he made possible. He gave me the Taj Mahal for my sixty-fifth birthday. What woman could ask for more than that?"

All the Single (Elder) Ladies

There are a lot of us. Some are widowed, some divorced, or, like myself, never married. Many don't have family, or, if they do, they can't necessarily depend on them. You hit a certain age and begin thinking about where you will live as you get older and with whom.

In the last twenty years, the divorce rate among baby boomers has increased by 50 percent. Men and women in their fifties and sixties are choosing to stay single. I've often talked with women friends about the idea of getting a big house to share; we would each have our own room, plus there would be communal living and dining area. What's your Aging Alone Plan? This decade is a good time to explore this. (For more information, see page 215.)

Social media is the ideal tool for elders, and the benefits are enormous. It has transformed the way families can stay in touch and share photos and videos. With Skype, grandparents can interact with kids whom they might not see on regular basis and visit with old friends who don't travel. And for sheer safety, cell phones and texting make it easy to communicate. It's also a great way to learn, grow a business, and even find work.

According to the Pew Research Center, Internet use among those sixty-five and older grew 150 percent between 2009 and 2011, the largest growth in a demographic group (*Huffington Post,* March 7, 2016).

Maggie Kuhn

In 1970, at age sixty-five, Maggie Kuhn was forced to retire from a job she loved. Fueled by her outrage and her passionate belief that "old people and women constituted America's biggest untapped and undervalued human energy source," she founded the Gray Panthers, creating one of the most powerful social movements of the century; one that advocated for nursing home reform, fought against ageism, and was committed to justice and peace for all, regardless of age.

Kuhn was a big proponent of intergenerational housing and shared her home with several young women in exchange for their help with chores. She received the support she needed along with youthful energy; they were the beneficiaries of her wisdom. It was a win-win and a concept that we could use today.

Chris Zydel

Chris offers workshops at her facility, Painting from the Wild Heart, nestled in magnificent settings, such as Ghost Ranch in New Mexico and the High Sierras in northern California. Her workshops are not just about making art; it's about the healing power of the creative process; expressing yourself, being seen, accepted and deeply valued.

"My dear friend, Julie Stuart, celebrated my sixtieth birthday here at Ghost Ranch," Chris said. "And she asked me to give her one word that characterized my fifties. The word that immediately came to mind was *dismantling*. During that decade, I felt like so much of who I thought I was had been stripped away for all different kinds of reasons. My bones had been picked clean of attitudes, beliefs, and ways of being that I identified as me. But that no longer served. And the word that I am left with to define my entrance into my sixties? Freedom. Sweet, delicious, no-holds-barred Freedom."

SARK

Susan Ariel Rainbow Kennedy is an artist, teacher, and author of seventeen books (*Living Juicy, Wild Succulent Love,* etc.). She conducts amazing webinars and online programs on writing, creativity, and manifesting, as well as personal mentoring. Her energy is contagious and deeply nourishing. Many introductory online seminars are free. Sign up for her delicious newsletter at Planet SARK.

Fabulous and Flawed!

Seeing gorgeous sixty-, seventy-, and eighty-year-old models walking the runway during Fashion Week and appearing in *Vogue;* celebrities writing anti-aging books; and photos of ninety-year-old yogis doing headstands on Facebook can feel intimidating.

I finally felt that I didn't have to prove myself, and now there's a new pressure to be old, fashionable, and relevant! Sounds exhausting. Sometimes you just want "a cuppa and a lie down," as they say in England. The answer? Perfection is overrated. We need to give ourselves permission to be both fabulous *and* flawed!

THE SEVENTIES
Real Problems, Real Possibilities

I am more myself than ever.
—May Sarton (at age 70)

This chapter is different from the others. Except for the Saturn opposition, the Jupiter Return, and Uranus sextile, there are no other major cycles during our seventies. As always, there are personal aspects but none of the generational ones. Nevertheless, this is an important decade, because it gives us an opportunity to find a way to embody this elder status and come to terms with the aging process. The lack of challenging aspects during this time can help us stabilize our life and our health—physical, mental, and emotional.

There's the sixth Jupiter Return between seventy-one and seventy-two, along with the harmonious sextile of Uranus to its natal position. Both of these aspects are supportive and uplifting and give us a boost as we enter this new decade. Uranus and Jupiter are sky gods, so this period can bring a more expansive perspective, a bigger world view, and a desire to learn.

Jupiter rules travel, so it's not unusual for people to either move (often to a foreign country) or to go on a cruise. Jupiter is also associated with religion, spirituality, and ceremonies. My nephew, Evan, got married during my Jupiter Return, and he and his fiancée, Becca, asked me to officiate at the wedding, which was very meaningful for me.

Diana Vreeland was seventy when she took the job as special consultant at the Costume Institute at the Metropolitan Museum. When asked why she accepted the position, she replied: "What was I supposed to do, retire? I was only seventy."

Singer Darlene Love appeared in *20 Feet from Stardom,* the Academy Award–winning documentary about back-up singers.

May Sarton published her journal, *At Seventy.*

Academy Award–winning actor Dustin Hoffman directed his first film, *Quartet,* in his early seventies. Interestingly, the film takes place in a retirement home for former musicians and deals with issues of aging.

At age seventy, singer/songwriter Sixto Rodriguez finally found success in America, where his music was virtually unknown. In 2013, the documentary about him, *Searching for Sugarman,* won an Academy Award.

Oliver Sacks fell in love for the first time in his seventies.

The Third Stage of Eldering: Here Comes Karma

Between seventy-two and seventy-three, we come to the Saturn opposition; Saturn is exactly opposite its birth position. This is the third and final stage of the elder cycle and signals an important threshold. Still, we're not finished with Saturn. At eighty, we have the closing square; and at eighty-eight, we have the third Saturn Return, but by that time we will be in the territory of old age. At this point, it's necessary to accept our elder standing with grace and good will.

The seeds of the elder we are to become are planted at our Second Saturn Return. At this stage, there can be a genuine flowering of the elder archetype and an opportunity to share the knowledge and the respect we've honed. By now, we've had a lot of experience dealing with the Great Teacher, and hopefully we've learned a thing or two. If we haven't already done so, it's time to make Saturn our friend; perhaps that's the real gift of this phase. We are still on this plateau between middle age and old age, and it is important to take advantage of it. And, yes, this decade has real problems, but there are also new possibilities and potential.

The Decade of Consequences

At the Saturn opposition, we have to deal with the consequences of the choices we've made; choices concerning our health, finances, family, our attitude, our self-care or lack of it. This can be a time of reckoning but also an opportunity to clean up our act.

By seventy, our habits are firmly established, sometimes too firmly, but that doesn't mean we can't continue to grow. We can create new habits at any age, but when we do it during a Saturn period, there's an excellent chance those behaviors will become an integral part of our lives.

During Saturn times, we often have experiences that expose our frailties; yet it's only by confronting and dealing with those areas that we can strengthen them. I think of Saturn as the contractor you call in to do some remodeling on your home. He or she may discover the problems are more complex, that they'll take longer and cost more. But by getting the work done, you are not only upgrading your home, you're making it stronger and more secure. We also get to see the results of what we began in our Saturn Return fourteen years ago.

Just as in our earlier Saturn opposition at forty-four, there can be growth, achievement, and success. If not, what do we need to do now to ensure a better future? What can we do now to improve our health, our finances, and our relationships? Once again, it's back to the drawing board; a time to review and reevaluate.

At this age, there are bound to be losses. Who hasn't lost a partner, family member, or close friend as a result of a long illness, an accident, or something catastrophic? Who hasn't had a health issue or a health scare? Who hasn't experienced some kind of financial crisis or had a change in circumstances? There are regrets and fears that can wear us down.

None of these are written in stone; none of this is a prediction; it simply comes with the territory of age. Grieving is a natural process, so it's necessary to go through it and not around it. Having support, community, and a way to share your feelings makes all the difference. In this technological world we now live in, the Internet can provide a place to do that.

Susan Ariel Rainbow Kennedy (SARK) lost her beloved partner, John Waddell, in March 2015. She is not in her seventies, but losses can happen at any age. By sharing her grieving/healing process honestly and openly online, she is guiding us all. Here is an excerpt from one of her posts:

> I'm actively deeply grieving while wildly living, and creating my wonder~full new life. Some days and parts of days, this goes better than others.

Here are a few of my grieving practices:

- I cry super hard and exaggerate the experience until it shifts and I feel a calm feeling come down all around me, and then relax. And sometimes it doesn't work.

- I'm doing a lot of self-hugging, multiple times in a day. And sometimes I just lie there helplessly.

- I'm allowing ALL my feelings, which is messy, inconvenient and initially rough. Still, I know it works better than sedating, anesthetizing or avoiding—which of course I also sometimes do.

I am remembering that healing happens in spirals and layers, not in steps like a ladder.

Thank you for being with me on my grieving and living journey —SARK

I learned about the work of Christina Rasmussen from SARK. People say that time heals, and that's certainly a part of the healing process, but Christina takes it further. Her Life Reentry process, based on neuroplasticity, "focuses on consciously releasing the pain in ways that both honor suffering and rewire the brain to change your perception of the world and yourself." Her book (*Second Firsts: Live, Laugh, and Love Again*) and her online community are wonderful resources.

Sheryl Sandberg's commencement speech to Berkeley's class of 2016 was a poignant testimony to both the power of grief and resilience. "When life sucks you under, you can kick against the bottom, find the surface, and breathe again," she said. "The question is not if some of these things will happen to you. They will." She went on to add, that you are "defined not just by what you achieve but how you survive."

Me at Seventy

One day I woke up and there was a seventy-year-old woman in my bed.
—Gloria Steinem

I believe there's a birthday for all of us when the whole aging thing really hits. It's usually one of the big ones: fifty, sixty, or sixty-five. For me it was seventy. Maybe because I've always looked younger than my actual age, and I'm in pretty good shape physically. Or more likely, it's because I have a tendency to be in denial. To tell you the truth, I was not thrilled about turning seventy. I just couldn't get my head around it. I suddenly realized that I'm not just getting older; I *am* old! How the hell did that happen?

My fifties were fabulous and totally liberating. My sixties were a genuine surprise. Everything seemed to come together; I felt calmer and saner than I ever had. But seventy? This was entering a foreign territory, and it seemed bleak and uninviting. In the 1960s, I traveled from Belgrade to Moscow by train in the dead of winter. There was a town in the Ukraine where the train stopped for several hours because the tracks from that point on were different, and the wheels on the train had to be adjusted accordingly. Turning seventy felt similar, except it seemed that the tracks themselves ended. How would I continue? Who would I be? I was concerned others would look at me differently, as if I had a tattoo on my face that screamed "old." People would judge me. I wouldn't be trendy or hip. Who was I kidding? I've never been trendy or hip.

It dawned on me that the problem wasn't my age, it was my attitude. I was judging myself the way I was afraid others would judge me. That shocked and saddened me and made me reexamine my own beliefs about aging. What I was doing was another form of beating myself up. I decided I had come too far to do that to myself.

The word *ageism* was coined in 1969 by Robert Butler, the same psychiatrist and gerontologist who created the life review. In her small but very fine book, *How to Age,* Anne Karpf writes about ageism being "prejudice against our future self." It keeps us in denial and disconnects us from the elder we will become. In a sense, it is like autoimmune disease; the body attacks itself. Karpf suggests, "We need to re-humanize older people."

Old age has been stigmatized to the point that we tend to project all our worst fears on the aged. We envision them—and our Western culture has enabled this—stooped and frail with low energy and libidos, then distance ourselves from them. This is not just harmful to the old; it is damaging to all ages. Reclaiming those feelings we project on the aged helps to break the cycle of ageism.

In *This Chair Rocks: A Manifesto Against Ageism,* author Ashton Applewhite reminds us that "only 4 percent of Americans over sixty-five live in nursing homes" and only 10 percent of those over eighty-five. One third of people seventy-five and older live alone. "Over half of 'the oldest old'—ages eighty-five and up—can go about their everyday activities without any personal assistance." In addition, many people in their sixties and seventies are caretakers themselves.

> *Your mindset can affect how you age.*
> —*Time* magazine, February 2016

How we view aging and the beliefs we have about getting older influences how we age. The words we use, even jokingly, about such things as "senior moments," send a negative message. Or repeating blanket statements like, "Our metabolism slows down as we age; it's harder to lose weight as you get older." That's not true for everyone. And this isn't simply New Age rhetoric. "For the first time, two studies published late last year in the journal *Psychology and Aging* linked a person's negative stereotypes about aging, of all things, to the development of brain changes associated with Alzheimer's disease."[26]

Dr. Christiane Northrup writes in her book *Goddesses Never Age:* "Mental habits play a huge role in our health and longevity." She references several studies. One of them is the well-known University of Minnesota longitudinal study of nuns, which began in 1986. The Nun Study is considered by experts on aging to be one of the best in terms of determining who gets Alzheimer's and why.

On entering the convent, each nun, all in their early twenties, wrote an autobiographical essay. The researchers discovered that the nuns who expressed more positive emotions when they were young experienced longevity (and were less likely to get Alzheimer's) than the ones who experienced more negative emotions. This study established clear links between attitude and longevity.

The most important thing you need to know about your health is that the health of your body and its organs does not exist separate from your emotional well-being, your thoughts, your cultural programming, and your spiritual outlook. Your thoughts and beliefs are the single most important indicator of your state of health.
—Christiane Northrup, *Goddesses Never Age*

Jamie Lee Curtis has the right idea. She gave an interview in 2016 that I read on Sixty and Me. She was fifty-seven years old at

---

[26]Alexandra Sifferlin, "Longevity: It's the Little Things That Keep Us Young," *Time* (Feb. 11, 2016).

the time. She said: "If I can challenge old ideas about aging, I will feel more and more invigorated. I want to represent this new way. I want to be a new version of the seventy-year-old woman. Vital, strong, very physical, very agile. I think that the older I get, the more yoga I'm going to do."

That is the kind of attitude that empowers your future self. What beliefs do you have about aging? Can you see a connection between your beliefs and how you're aging? Do you tell yourself: "I'm too old; it's too late; I don't have the education or the credentials?" Become conscious of what you tell yourself. This decade of the seventies is a great time to reframe those beliefs.

My Saturn Opposition at Seventy-Two

As I write this book, I am experiencing this Saturn transit, and let me tell you, it's turned out to be a colossal reality check; not all bad but definitely not easy. One thing I am really, really good at is procrastinating, and Saturn has forced me confront a number of things I had been successfully avoiding for a long time.

For many years, I've had an underactive thyroid that I healed by going 100 percent gluten-free. The results from a recent blood test showed my thyroid was normal, but now there was something wrong with my parathyroid. Para what? I didn't even know such an organ existed.

At the time, Saturn was in Sagittarius and only approaching the opposition to my natal Saturn (in Gemini). I had to take a whole series of tests. At the same time, I got talked into taking some other basic tests that I had dodged for years, like a mammogram and a bone density test. In the end, my parathyroid turned out to be fine; it just functions differently, and there's a category for that.

I did discover that I had bone loss (Saturn rules bones), which was discouraging. I decided to approach it naturally, and I've been rigorous with supplements and exercise. I started taking ballet, which is very structured, very Saturn (not to mention extremely humbling). I also began attending an exercise class at my gym to build up my core strength.

In fact, the term "core strength" is a great metaphor for a Saturn transit. It involves doing certain exercises to strengthen our core muscles—abdominal muscles, back muscles, and the muscles around the pelvis, which stabilize the body during movement. In a sense, we are strengthening our foundation, which is what Saturn asks us to do.

When Saturn was exactly opposite its natal position, I had some dental surgery that I had been putting off. At the same time, I had to deal with a health insurance problem; a chore even less appealing then dental surgery. I also handled some financial issues. In addition, I sold a number of antiques (that I had no room for) at an auction; something else I had been postponing. Just getting them out of my apartment cleared the air and shifted the energy. In fact, facing all of these problems was extremely empowering for me.

There's no growth in the comfort zone and no comfort in the growth zone.
—author unknown

It was during my Saturn opposition that I got the opportunity to publish this book. Now I love a good deadline (I tend to drift without one), but this one was tight, and it brought up my worst fears: Can I do this? Will I be able to complete it in time? Will I be judged? At times, I've felt overwhelmed and not up to the task. Saturn has definitely pushed, sometimes dragged, me way outside my comfort zone, forcing me to become more disciplined and focused. This has turned out to be the year of reality and thanks to the Lord of Karma, I'm stronger as a result.

My Age Finally Fits Me!

This year, Saturn has helped me to really embrace my age. Not like when I as in my fifties and sixties and I looked a decade younger, but embracing myself now, when I actually look my age. In *How to Age,* Anne Karpf quotes a woman who says: "I am sixty-three years old and for the first time in my life, I feel my age fits me." When I read that, I wanted to jump up and down. "That's me, damn it!" I exclaimed. I actually like being this age; it feels right, natural. I'm a good older person. I was never good at being young; I was miserable.

For me, getting older hasn't been hard. What was really hard was being young, stupid, and scared and having absolutely no skills or support. When I was young, everything seemed like a major crisis. What age has given me is more perspective, a longer fuse, a wider view. It doesn't mean that I don't have problems, issues, or fears; sure I do, but what I don't have is the drama. And while I may not be proud of all the choices I've made in my life, I'm at peace with them. What I am proud of is the way I've turned out. I may not be the star I dreamed of becoming, but I'm also not the train wreck I feared I would turn into. My life isn't ideal (whose is?), but I am grateful for every little thing. I take nothing for granted.

Fifty Years of Dieting and Exercise: What I've Learned (It's Not Complicated)

I'm not a health professional, nutritionist, or therapist; I have no advanced degrees; in fact, I've never gone to college. I've failed at many things: businesses, relationships, finances—you name it.

What I have going for me is that I love to learn. As a result, I've explored, experienced, and studied many therapies, spiritual practices, and disciplines.

Having owned a health-food restaurant for twenty years, I've learned a great deal about food and nutrition. Along the way, I've healed my eating disorder, overcome low self-esteem—or, as I like to say, *no* self-esteem—repaired my relationship with my father (no small thing), and, after years of being angry, fearful, and sad, I've learned to love myself and be happy. I may be road weary and a little ragged about the edges, but overall I'm in pretty good shape. I rest my case. It has taken me a long time to get to this place. This is what I've learned.

Attitude: Attitude isn't the only thing, it's *everything*. It is the engine that runs the whole shebang! You can eat the purest organic foods, exercise every day, and drink pristine water and lots of green juice, but if you're miserable, angry, and anxious, your health will suffer anyway, not to mention your looks. Your attitude is your foundation; everything else is built on it. I believe that if a diet or exercise plan isn't based on self-love, self-respect, and self-care, it ultimately doesn't work. Oh, you can get skinny, strong, and flexible, but that doesn't mean you will be healed. I learned the hard way.

Consistency: You don't have to do extreme sports or excessive dieting and fasting. In fact, it's best if you don't. You do have to be consistent. That doesn't mean perfect. If you fail, you forgive yourself and begin again. A plane flying from New York to Los Angeles is off course 95 percent of the time, yet the plane arrives at its destination. Why? Thanks to sophisticated systems, the plane keeps communicating information to the pilot, who then makes corrections. You just keep adjusting. Like recovery work, it's one day at a time or even one hour at a time. *Small changes done consistently over time will produce solid results.*

Keep It Simple!: It's not rocket science. What you put in your body, on your skin, and *especially* in your mind needs to be wholesome, nontoxic, and nutritious. Diet sodas, sugar substitutes, and many frozen desserts may be low in calories, but they contain chemicals that can interfere with your digestion. Violent movies can disrupt sleep patterns. Sugar is a drug. Personally, I wouldn't have Botox or fillers injected in my face. But hey, I'm a double Taurus; I'd rather spend that money on a vacation. But more to the point, let's see the long-term effects.

Food: There is no one diet for everyone. In fact, forget diet altogether; it contains the word *die.* You have to find a food plan that works for you personally; *a plan for life,* a plan for your relationship with food. It's a very personal thing. Some people thrive on a macrobiotic or vegan diet; others don't. Some people need more protein; other people do well with less. You make allowances for special treats and occasional indulgences because this is not for just two or three weeks; this is not a quick fix, you're in it for the long haul. You need the faith of Jupiter but the work and self-discipline is pure Saturn. If you stay with it, the result will be Venusian.

If you think the pursuit of good health is
expensive and time consuming, try illness.
—Lee Swanson

Years ago, I went to an enlightened naturopath named Dr. James D'Adamo; his diet, based on blood types, changed my life. Food combining makes total sense to me. This is a centuries-old way of eating that optimizes the process of digestion. It is based on the concept that different foods digest at different speeds and therefore should be combined accordingly. For instance, fruit should be eaten alone and on an empty stomach. Green and non-starchy vegetables can be eaten with either protein or starch. But protein and grains should not be eaten together. Many of the countries where people live the longest eat this way naturally.

I learned about eating water soluble foods from Tony Robbins—foods, like vegetables and fruits, that cleanse your body. One of the main things that helped me was eating the same quantity of food over a long period of time. Learning what kinds of food were beneficial was essential. Therapy was a huge part of the recipe, as was body work. But the most important ingredient was learning to love myself, and that took time.

Exercise: We all know that "sitting is the new smoking." You need to move; you don't need to suffer. Find something you love to do; it doesn't matter what—bicycling, aerobic classes, yoga, chair yoga, Pilates, dance, swimming. Or just take a hike. Research shows "creative problem solving can be improved by disconnecting from technology and reconnecting with nature." Don't make yourself crazy. Do it a few times a week. Like anything, if you fall off, get back on. Don't judge. Start where you are, do what you can. Keep going.

Like a food plan, an exercise program has to be right for you. Even if you haven't been physically active, it's not too late. An English Longitudinal Study on Ageing shows that "older adults who started to exercise even once a week—even after being inactive—were three to four times more likely to age healthily compared to their continuously inactive peers."[27]

Exercise actually promoted gene activity that
lowers beta-amyloid levels in the brain.
—Super Brain (Deepak Chopra and Rudolph E. Tanzi)

Personally, I love to exercise; it's my Prozac without a prescription—it clears my head. There were times in my late teens and twenties when I was obsessive; I took several dance classes a day and then worked at night as a dancer in clubs. Now I go to the gym a few times a week. On other days, I walk at least an hour a day or take a ballet class. I try to swim when possible. Sometimes, if I don't have time, I run into the gym for a "quickie"—twenty minutes on the treadmill and ten or fifteen minutes of weights, and I'm out of there. It's not about doing a lot; *it's about doing a little over a long period of time.*

During the 1970s, Jean Houston spoke at a class at the New School for Social Research about how a person walking around New York City for one day had more stimulation than someone a hundred years ago had in their entire lifetime. That was before personal computers, the Internet, and cell phones. Where does all that information and mental debris go? The practice of fêng shui encourages clearing out clutter to create harmony in our physical environment. What about the clutter we hoard in our head? It doesn't matter whether you meditate, spend time in nature, or just allow yourself to be quiet; what's important is to find a way

---

[27]Yagana Shah, "Starting Exercise Even Later in Life Triples Chance of Aging Healthily," *Huffington Post* (Nov. 26, 2013).

each day to let go of yourself and your ego, and drop into a more expansive and forgiving place.

My Own Spiritual Routine

Every morning, I get up, make myself a cup of organic coffee, light a few candles, and sit down at my living room table. Around the room are statues of Kwan Yin, Buddha, Mary, goddesses, and altars with sacred object and photographs of my spiritual teachers, guides, and friends. I write in my journal, meditate, pray, and set my intentions for the day. My practice is definitely more funky than formal, but it suits me. It's my favorite part of the day.

~~~~~~

Meditation

Mindfulness meditation can reduce stress and prevent people from ruminating in negative emotions, and some form of meditation practice may even slow the biological signs of aging by stabilizing telomeres. (*Time*, Longevity Issue, February 6, 2016)

~~~~~~

Silence Please! "A 2013 study on mice published in the journal *Brain, Structure, and Function* used different types of noise and silence and monitored the effect the sound and silence had on the brains of the mice. . . . The scientists discovered that when the mice were exposed to two hours of silence per day, they developed new cells in the hippocampus. The hippocampus is the region of the brain associated with memory, emotion, and learning."[28]

---

[28]Rebecca Beris, "Science Says Silence Is Much More Important to Our Brains Than We Think," Lifehack website, *www.lifehack.org*.

Skin: Good, pure products are essential, as are regular facials; but ultimately it's not what goes on your face but what goes into your body. What you eat, drink, smoke, and even think shows up on your face eventually. Choose carefully.

Plastic surgery and other procedures can make you look younger, but at what cost? You are "stopping the clock," which, to me, sends a message that you are no longer growing or maturing. I understand and respect the desire to look your best, but if you are going to have surgery done, be sure to explore the reasons. If there are self-esteem issues or body issues, then it's best to get some therapy or counselling first.

Facial acupuncture is both effective and noninvasive, plus it has been around for five thousand years. It works on balancing the organs, especially the liver, which has a great deal to do with the overall aging process. Facial acupuncture strengthens the internal system, which is then reflected in the outer appearance. Mary Elizabeth Wakefield, facial acupuncturist and author of *Constitutional Facial Acupuncture,* says, "Constitutional Facial Acupuncture is both an ancient art and a revolutionary treatment that links inner beauty and radiance with outer physical balance."

Pleasure: "Experiencing pleasure is crucial to vibrant health," wrote D. Christiane Northrup. We are not here to suffer; we are here to live fully and live juicy.

In the end, it comes down to the little things we do. It's not running five miles every day, meditating for hours, or eating only vegan or gluten-free.

The latest science is showing quite the opposite, in fact: that extending healthy life is attainable for many of us with just a few small changes that aren't especially hard to do—and won't make you miserable. . . . [Not just working out in] the gym . . . but . . . fidgeting. . . . *Finally, they are convinced that your inner life has an important impact on how well the body ages on a biological level.*[29] (italics mine)

One of the most damaging things we can do (in my opinion) is to label every health concern, memory slip, and liver spot as a sign that we are quickly skidding into old age, illness, and dementia. We act like those high-priced lawyers on television shows who are building a case—except it's against ourselves! Don't make your-self into a "person of interest," as they say on the detective shows. That doesn't mean we should ignore signs or symptoms; not at all. Maybe that buzzing in your ear is tinnitus; do see a doctor about the mole on your arm or the chronic pain in your hip. Have your eyes and hearing checked.

But don't sentence yourself before all the evidence has been presented and the jury has made a decision. Worrying about things before they happen is like praying for your problems. And sure, it's easy to say, but that kind of thinking is a habit, and, like all habits, you can change it.

There Really Is a Fountain of Youth

You won't find youth in a luxurious scented cream displayed in an expensive bottle at Bergdorf Goodman or in a potion invented at a dermatologist's office, having a medical name and pristine packaging. It doesn't come in a pill, an injection, or a five-hundred-dollar facial given by someone with a single name and a six-month

---

[29]Sifferlin, "Longevity," *Time* (Feb. 11, 2016).

waiting list. You don't have to travel to a spa in Switzerland or a secret location in Chinatown or to the shores of the Black Sea. And you won't find youth on one of those infomercials you see at three in the morning. The solution costs nothing and lasts forever.

It's not enough to accept your age. You must surrender to your age. Aging beautifully requires that we embrace it, cherish it, and stand in awe of its influence.
—Ilene Cummings, author of *The Lavender Lace Bra*

The fountain of youth is inside *you.* In fact, it says so in the word: *youth.* All you have to do is be happy, feel good, be grateful, and love yourself. Oh, and forgive yourself and others. I know, it sounds like New Age thinking, a Pollyanna approach. I'm not saying it's easy. It's a lifetime process, an ongoing practice, so the earlier you begin, the better. It can't hurt, and it doesn't cost anything. There's absolutely no downside. It's good for your cell tissue, immune system, your heart rate, your organs, your skin, and your weight. It will give you a glow. It will help you sleep. It won't necessarily take away your wrinkles or age spots, but people won't notice, because they'll feel good in your presence.

One study found that people who have a positive outlook about aging live approximately seven and a half years longer than their glass-is-half-empty peers. Fearing aging, stressing over the symptoms of aging, and worrying about the downside of age can actually make the aging process more challenging.

How to Begin
Start by keeping a gratitude journal: Every day, write down a few things you're grateful for—the perfect latte, a walk in the rain, a great dinner with close friends. There are so many things we take

for granted, like our health, our eyes, our feet, the roof over our head, the food we eat. Personally, I believe that it's the big things that get us through life but the little ones that get us through the day, and it's about getting through the day!

Create a happiness jar: Author Elizabeth Gilbert is a huge fan of this wonderful ritual and writes about it on her website. At the end of the day she grabs a scrap of paper (a corner of a bill or an old list) and jots down her happiest moments, dates it, folds it, and sticks it in a jar. And that's all. The beauty of this practice is that it transforms you into a detective of happiness, a Sherlock of gladness; always on the look-out for something delightful to write about. It's subtle but deceptively empowering. And when you don't feel so terrific you can reach into your jar and read one of these notes. It will make you smile. I promise you.[30]

Focus on what's working instead of what's not working: Talk about what you want and not what you don't want. You don't have to do it 24/7 either, just for a few minute at a time several times a day. I do this on the treadmill, while I'm doing errands, and when I'm cleaning.

Make being happy a habit: I'm not talking about when life is smooth, and there are no problems or challenges (that's easy), but when things get rough, when crises hit. That's when it really counts. I love the book *Happy for No Reason,* but I love the title even more. What a concept! Being happy for absolutely no reason is like

---

[30]Elizabeth Gilbert, from her website: *www.elizabethgilbert.com.*

having a trust fund. You're set for life! As Voltaire famously said, "I have chosen to be happy because it's good for my health."

"Success leaves clues; so does failure": I remember Tony Robbins saying something similar to this in his seminars during the 1980s: Look around at the people who are fulfilled, happy, healthy, who have good relationships and work they love. What kind of attitude do they have? What are their habits? Study them, model them, learn from them.

Stories
Joel's Story
Joel has worked in the real estate business for thirty years; he leases commercial office space in New York City and has been successful. A few years ago, the company he worked for was sold, and he was out of work. Joel was in his early seventies at the time. Not exactly the best age to dive into the job market during a weak economy, but that's exactly what he did.

A classy man with youthful energy, he decided he wasn't ready to retire. He interviewed for several months and received three job offers. He decided on one and began work and has thrived there. That's a nice story but it gets better.

Joel has a godson in his twenties who wanted to get into the real estate business. Joel brought him into the company and began mentoring him. Joel was already fluent with computers, iPads, and iPhones, but his godson opened up the world of social media in terms of business. Together they make a great team and are empowering each other. This is a great example of intergenerational support.

You age because you cannot change.
—Ramtha

Hilda's Story

I'm still learning.
—Michelangelo, at age eighty-two

Hilda has been in the skin care business for more than sixty years. She gives a superb facial, and I always leave with my face glowing, but I also come for her nurturing energy and positive attitude.

As a young girl, her education was interrupted, so she didn't finish high school until her own children were in school. Yet she is constantly learning and growing. At seventy, Hilda enrolled in One Spirit seminary, an interfaith church, and became a minister—at the time of her Jupiter Return. Then at seventy-two, she decided she wanted to go to college—so she did! She earned her BA, MA, and a PhD!

Hilda's husband died, and she went into a slump. However, she received the support she needed and healed. She had attended a bereavement group at Memorial Sloan Kettering hospital. When it concluded, the other members asked her to start one, which of course she did. Hilda also counsels, officiates weddings, and continues to learn. When I last saw her, she was excited about a course that she was starting the following week. Hilda is eighty-three.

I can't understand why people are frightened of new ideas.
I'm frightened of the old ones.
—John Cage

Rose, the Sprout Lady

Years ago, when I owned my natural foods restaurant in New York City's West Village, I bought my alfalfa sprouts from a woman named Rose, who was affectionately referred to as Rose Sprout or the Sprout Lady. At my restaurant, we put alfalfa sprouts on practically everything: house salads, entrée salads, sandwiches; we even used them as a garnish on entrées, so we went through several huge bags a week.

Over the years, I got to know Rose; she was a vegetarian and a regular customer at the restaurant. I would often sit down and chat with her while she was having dinner. Rose had come to New York City from Germany, along with her husband, during the late 1930s. They had a business together and raised a family. After her husband died, Rose lived alone in her apartment on Fifth Avenue, just a block from my restaurant.

One day I asked her how she got into the sprout business. She told me that she lost all her money in the stock market in 1974. "So, vhat vas I to do, Virginia?" She spoke with a strong German Jewish accent. "I couldn't ask my children. One summer, my grandson vas visiting me. I saw him growing these alfalfa sprouts. I vatched vhat he vas doing and said to myself, 'Rose, you could do that!'" She was in her mid-seventies at the time.

Alfalfa sprouts require a lot of light, so she began growing them in jars on her kitchen windowsill; eventually, she graduated to growing them in large trays. She would put the finished sprouts in these giant plastic bags and wheel them to her customers in a shopping cart. As she got older, the cart served as a makeshift walker. Over the years, Rose developed quite a lucrative business; her customers were the health food restaurants in the West Village and SoHo, plus the upscale food markets in the neighborhood, such as Balducci's and Jefferson Market. She retired in her eighties with a nice little nest egg—made from alfalfa sprouts.

Rose was constantly learning and growing. She took classes and attended lectures at the New School for Social Research, just around the corner on 12th Street. A friend who knew Rose once spotted her at Omega Institute, the conference center in Rhinebeck, New York. A group of people were doing a trust-building exercise out on the lawn; they were lifting an older woman high above their heads and gently rocking her. The woman looked familiar, so my friend moved in closer; it was Rose. She was in her eighties.

Even My Dad Healed in His Seventies

Growing up, my father worked as a short-order cook in an all-night diner. He was constantly on his feet, ate on the run, and slept only a few hours during the day. He was either sullen or angry and explosive. Life improved once he retired and was no longer working crazy hours, commuting two hours each day, and taking pills to stay awake. With less pressure the anger subsided, but he still wasn't easy. A Sagittarius (not the enlightened kind), he had that "my way or the highway" kind of personality. Then I opened my restaurant.

Dad was seventy-three at the time and having his own Saturn opposition. I never asked him to come and help out; he just showed up that first day and started working. Four days a week, he took the Long Island train from Great Neck to Penn station—a twenty-five-minute ride; then he took the subway downtown. He arrived around seven in the morning, put on the coffee for the staff, and set up the dining room.

Then he would do prep for the lunch cooks—chopping mounds of onions and garlic. Afterward, he would set up the garnishes—parsley, sprouts, and the sunflower seeds that topped the salads. I told him he didn't have to come in so much or work so hard, but he insisted. "What am I going to do at home?" The truth is, he slept little and liked to be busy. He may have been angry and abusive when I was growing up, but he had a solid work ethic.

I had two lunch cooks in those early days, both women, and he adored them. Buffy was gentle and very spiritual and treated him with tremendous kindness. Angela, of Italian decent, was feisty, outspoken, and made fabulous soups. I would hear him talking with Angela in the kitchen, sotto voce. "What do you talk about with him?" I asked her. "He tells me about your mother, about his problems." I was shocked; I'd never had an actual conversation with my father my entire life, but he was confiding in Angela.

My father had never given me anything, and now he was making a real contribution. I felt that deeply. And the restaurant was also giving something back to him. Growing up, I never knew him to have any friends, but at the restaurant, he was engaging with people. The staff was young, and many of them were involved in some kind of spiritual path; they treated him with respect. Over time, I saw him soften. The restaurant was good for me in so many ways, but the most important thing it did was to help me have a relationship with my father. I thought I was building a business, but the restaurant was more than that. I was healing. So was my father.

THE URANUS RETURN AT EIGHTY-FOUR
The Homecoming

We shall not cease from exploration
And the end of all our exploring
Will be to arrive where we started
And know the place for the first time.
—T. S. Eliot, "Little Gidding"

We have come to the end of the generational cycles and the final chapter of this book. In all of the great stories, this is the time when the hero or heroine returns home. Like Odysseus finally reaching Ithaca, we come back to where we started; nothing has changed, yet we are different or hopefully more ourselves, "wealthy with all that you have gained on the way," as the Greek poet Constantine P. Cavafy wrote in his famous poem, "Ithaka."

The Saturn Square at Eighty

I'm looking forward to eighty.
—Oliver Sacks

At age eighty, we are beyond the cycle of eldering, although the process continues as long as we are alive. Now we enter the territory of old age, and it seems fitting that we are greeted once again by our old friend Saturn. Where Saturn goes, reality follows.

Once again, we are confronted with new limitations, constraints, and boundaries. Once again, we must take an accounting of our life and our circumstances. During earlier Saturn transits, there were restrictions but also new endeavors, even adventures. At eighty, we're not necessarily working toward a higher degree, beginning a new career, or raising a family. Some arrangements and activities and events that we had depended on may end or change. Many people at eighty can—or should—no longer drive, and that impacts their living situation dramatically.

Old friends die, and there are fewer opportunities to establish new relationships or interests, though this is certainly not impossible. One of the benefits of relocating to a retirement community or assisted living facility is the support system and interaction it offers. Once again, these are Saturn issues and require Saturn skills.

When my friend Sharon's mother was in her eighties, she failed her driving test. That was a big part of her decision to move to an assisted living community in Florida. Although she had reservations about such a community, the move proved to be a happy surprise. When I spoke to Sharon, she told me that the place was comfortable, the people were terrific, and her mother was thriving. She was even looking forward to visiting her mother in her lovely new home.

Judy's father, Hersh, had open heart surgery when he was eighty-five. At ninety, he had a pacemaker put in. Unfortunately, at the same time, his landlord was selling the building where he had lived for almost thirty years, and he had to give up his apartment. The good news is that he found a place across the street that was much nicer. The only problem was that Hersh is a scholar, and he had 125 *boxes* of books! Family and friends pitched in to help give most of the books away. As Judy told him, "You have all the knowledge inside you. Now you're ready for some new stories."

The Uranus Return

At each of the Uranus cycles—at 21 and 42 and 63 and 84—we get a new chance to answer the voice within us that calls for more unique individuality. Even at 84, when Uranus returns to its birth position, there's a part of us that opens up to ways of seeing things differently. Personal epiphanies abound at age 84 and people often notice a renewed sense of well-being and a feeling like a "breath of fresh air has come into their lives." Some people, such as Carl Jung and Joseph Campbell "completed" their lives at this time.
—Elizabeth Spring, astrologer and author, *The Saturn Returns*

Around the age of eighty-four, freedom-loving Uranus returns to its natal position. At this time, it has completed its journey around the chart and interacted with every single planet, awakening, arousing, stimulating, and hopefully transforming our consciousness and that area of the chart where the planet is located. We have come full circle; there is nothing left to prove. As Carl Jung might say, we have become *fully individualized.* This is a culmination of a life well lived and, simultaneously, a new beginning.

The word "retrospective" (*retro* means *back,* and *spect* means *to see*) implies contemplation of the past, a survey of previous times and events. If one has been living consciously, this can be the harvest of a fully realized life; a time of refining and distilling the essence of one's existence and bringing it into some kind of form.

It's a time for consolidating one's opus and leaving a legacy. It is no coincidence that many artists, writers, philosophers, and great thinkers have published their memoirs, had major exhibits, or did their best work at this age.

* Michelangelo was working at St. Peter's during his eighties

* Carl Jung wrote *Memories, Dreams, and Reflections*

* Georgia O'Keeffe had a retrospective at the Whitney Museum

* Joseph Campbell was interviewed by Bill Moyers for the series that became *The Power of Myth* that went on to inspire generations

* Frank Lloyd Wright completed the design of the Guggenheim Museum when he was eighty

* Doctor Seuss (Theodor Geisel) won a Pulitzer Prize

Chita Rivera, aged eighty-three, was honored at the 2016 Kennedy Center Awards, as was Cecily Tyson, then ninety-one. This was not the culmination of their careers. Both women continue to be active with starring roles on TV. Cecily Tyson starred on Broadway in 2016.

Did their creativity contribute to their longevity? It's well documented that conductors, musicians, and artists often live long lives. Among the long-lived are:

* Leopold Stokowski, who died at ninety-five

* Cellist Pablo Casals, who died at ninety-six

* Arturo Toscanini, who died at eighty-nine

* Pablo Picasso, who died at ninety-two.

Perhaps what kept these artistic titans going is that they had a passion in their lives and a fervent need to create and contribute. Plus, artists rarely "retire." Confined to a wheelchair after an accident, Italian film director Bernardo Bertolucci thought his film-making days were over. But he accepted his situation and continued to direct—*from his wheelchair.* His last film, *Me and You,* was released in 2012, when he was seventy-two.

In his later years, the artist Pierre-Auguste Renoir could no longer walk, and his fingers were stiff, but he continued to paint by attaching a paintbrush to his hand. These great individuals are inspiring because they remind us of what is possible in our own later years. Even if we're not prominent people with public roles, we can still flourish; it's just going to look different. We all have a life and a legacy that needs expressing and that can take many forms besides painting the Sistine Chapel or, like Verdi, composing Falstaff at eighty.

> *The universe is made of stories, not of atoms.*
> —Muriel Rukeyser

In older times, the elders in the tribe passed on their wisdom through an oral tradition. It was their task to educate the clan through stories, music, and ceremonies. In a sense, that tradition is being revived today through the Internet. We live in a digital age, in which you can use your iPhone as a video camera to record a friend's or relative's stories or have them record yours. Self-publishing makes it easy to bring one's story into the world.

Blogging is accessible. This is living history that needs to be preserved. In addition to providing priceless information for one's family, it's also empowering for the person telling the story.

This process of harvesting one's life; surveying the past, gathering one's experiences together in a kind of narrative, brings a sense of completion. Because there are fewer expectations and less ego involved, there is also less pressure. It is a powerful exercise and a deeply satisfying process. One of the gifts of Uranus is the freedom to reclaim parts of ourselves, and this "harvesting" can help bring that about. By the way, Uranus also rules technology.

Having a retrospective or writing your memoir sounds wonderful, but at this age we know it's not the whole story. The planet Uranus is a wild card; it disturbs the status quo and shakes things up.

* We met Uranus at twenty-one, when it fueled our youthful rebellion.

* We experienced its full force at midlife, when Uranus opposed itself and an old life was shattered.

* In our early sixties, Uranus made its closing square, and once again we were encouraged to expand our horizons.

However, the conjunction we experience at age eighty-four is the most powerful aspect. We are no longer in our forties or even sixties. What happens now? Having come full circle, we are beyond the cycle of ambition—the ego's job is done. We may have work we love, but at this point in our lives, that desire arises from an inner need and not an outer demand. Having reached this point, there can be a feeling, not of disinterest but a rich detachment.

When Uranus is present, change is never far away, and a move is not uncommon at this age—either to a retirement home somewhere with a warmer climate, or into some kind of living situation with relatives. Independence is important at any age and never more so than when we reach our eighties. Having freedom and choices is essential to our well-being. The aging population is enormous, and thanks to the baby boomers, it's getting bigger, which means there will be new and better solutions.

For instance, "aging in place" enables seniors over sixty-five to live in their own home and community safely, independently, and comfortably, regardless of age, income, or ability. Granny Pods are tiny guest houses with medical extras; the little buildings can be installed in the backyard. There are currently twenty-three million Americans who are taking care of their elderly parents; Granny Pods offer autonomy for both the caregiver and the senior.

In Paris, there is Babayaga's House, a feminist alternative to an old-age home that began in 2013. One quarter of the seventeen million people in France are over the age of sixty; by 2050, that will be one third.

And in Helsinki, where rents are high, a nursing home offers inexpensive studios to Millennials. The young people get reduced rents; the elderly residents have an opportunity to mix with an age group they rarely have contact with. The program has been a huge success. In the Netherlands, a retirement home offers rent-free housing to university students who agree to volunteer thirty hours per month. These are exciting programs, and hopefully they'll become a trend.

New York magazine's 2014 cover story about old age in the Big Apple made an excellent case for retiring in New York City, assuming one has an affordable apartment. You don't need a car, which is a big plus, as the transit system is excellent; and you have all the cultural accouterments, such as museums, theaters, and movies that offer senior discounts. Plus, colleges like Fordham and Columbia have special senior classes. It's better than Boca!

Are You Weird Enough?

Many people at this age become true eccentrics. Let's face it, the older we get, hopefully the less self-conscious we are about speaking up and being ourselves. If you've always played by the rules (*especially* if you've played by the rules), you may become more outspoken and have fewer filters and more truth. It's often said that "age is the great liberator," and this is a time when you may be ready to become a delightfully unconventional older person.

The Old English word *wyrd* means "destiny." This late Middle English adjective originally meant "having the power to control destiny." It famously describes the Weird Sisters; originally, this referred to the Fates and later to the witches in Shakespeare's play *Macbeth*.

In his book *Fate and Destiny,* Michael Meade wrote about how important it is for true elders to be weird. "Elders are supposed to be weird, not simply 'weirdos,' but strange and unusual in a meaningful way." If you are seeking an elder, he suggests, look for someone who is "weird enough to become wise."

The Neptune Opposition

Howard Sasportas wrote in *The Gods of Change,*

> Neptune opposing its own place does not have to leave us confused, bitter and full of regrets. Through the kind of introspection and soul-searching transiting. Neptune invokes at this time, we are capable of achieving not only

a healthier level of self-esteem, but also a greater respect for that higher ordering principal, both mysterious and wise, which guides and oversees all our lives.[31]

Neptune, which we encountered in the midlife chapter, is the planet of the invisible world. It is the Poseidon, the Greek god of the sea, and rules all that is beneath our conscious awareness. Neptune is pure consciousness. Its domain is water; it is elusive, porous, and mystical.

When we reach this age, Neptune can bring a longing for a connection with the Divine or, if that already exists, a deepening of that relationship. There can be a greater respect for the sacred and for that which guides and governs our lives. It's what author, poet, and philosopher John O'Donohue calls "coming home to our deeper nature."

Neptune is associated with compassion, and this transit can bring more empathy. As our lives become simpler and our responsibilities in the world lessen, we have more time to reflect and contemplate. Neptune reminds us that it's not a failure to slow down; embracing our age and our abilities frees us to find new and gentler ways to be in the world. Neptune's gift at this time is that it allows us to open, soften, and receive.

Neptune is also associated with sacrifice. Neptune works by dissolving and washing things away, so this transit can also coincide with a time of fading memory and physical weakness. Neptune doesn't cause these things, but it does bring them to the surface. The loss of short-term memory and a propensity to forget names can increase during this period. It is natural for the brain to

---

[31]Howard Sasportas, *The Gods of Change: Pain, Transits and the Transits of Uranus, Neptune and Pluto* (London: Penguin Group, 1989), p. 143.

go through a cyclical pruning process. We have to be careful and not assume this is a given.

Author and physician Oliver Sacks wrote an essay entitled "My Own Life" that was published in the *New York Times* op-ed section on February 19, 2015, six months before his death.[32] His cancer had spread, and he knew his time was limited. Transiting Neptune was exactly opposite his natal Neptune, and the tone of his essay expresses the humanity and benevolence of this planet.

I love how honest and open he is about his illness and his fear but his "predominant feeling" is gratitude. He feels lucky that he has had the privilege to live past eighty, publish books, travel, and experience love. He writes that he feels "intensely alive" and wants to spend what time he has left deepening his friendships, writing, and perhaps even having fun. He lived a rich, meaningful, and conscious life right up to the end.

Uranus, Neptune, and Jupiter
Older and Wiser

At midlife, in our early forties, we experienced both the edgy intensity of high-voltage Uranus and the dissolving effect of watery Neptune, and we've seen how confusing but also how fruitful a time that is. Once again, these two great gods are in our lives, but now we're older and less robust.

Uranus is lightning; Neptune is fog. Uranus is sudden; Neptune slow. Yet this collaboration can bring about a genuine exploration of meaning along with a desire to bring all the pieces of our life together. The result can be real wisdom, the gift of Jupiter at this seventh Return. One of the things available to us no matter

---

[32]Oliver Sacks, "My Own Life," *New York Times* (Feb. 19, 2015).

what our circumstances or health is the exploration of what genuine wisdom is to each of us. The adventure of going deeper, experiencing the fullness of our life, and integrating as much as humanly possible. At midlife, we began to ask the big questions. Perhaps now we have some of the answers.

Old Age

You're Only Old Once!
—Dr. Seuss, the title of his book published on his eighty-second birthday

When I'm searching for inspiration on weighty subjects, such as life, death, and old age, I often turn to John O'Donohue and his book *Anam Cara: A Book of Celtic Wisdom.* The Celtic perspective includes the physical plane as well as the eternal. It contains great fluidity and poetry and a deep reverence for the unknown, the unfamiliar, and the mysterious. In *Anam Cara,* O'Donohue has written with great tenderness about the aging process.

> Old age can be a wonderful time to develop the art of inner harvesting. . . . The beauty and invitation of old age offer a time of silence and solitude for a visit to the house of your inner memory.[33]

When exactly is old age? Today young people seem older and wiser and older people are more youthful. More and more, our role models in their eighties are vigorous and active, still working, still thriving. And while it's important to keep it real, it's also important to remember what's possible.

---

[33]John O'Donohue, *Anam Cara: A Book of Celtic Wisdom* (New York: HarperCollins, 1997), pp. 173, 181.

Astrologer Shirley Soffer sees clients most days, publishes articles, lectures, and conducts her regular Wednesday night class. She told me recently that since turning eighty, she has become more self-assured, caring less about what others think and relying more on her intuition and experience.

* Hilda has her facial clients, conducts weddings, counsels people, and is constantly studying new areas.

* At eighty-six, Bodhi Hanna Kistner still teaches Kyudo, Japanese Zen archery.

* Louise Hay, at ninety, is motivating a whole new generation through her books, lectures, and online community.

* Gloria Steinem, who published her memoir, *My Life on the Road,* at eighty-one, continues to be a firebrand.

What Works: I believe the older we get, the lighter we need to travel. We need to let go of the material stuff that weighs us down but also the regrets, grudges, and negativity that is so damaging. If we haven't already done so, it's time to make peace with the past, with others, and with ourselves. Don't let your past determine your present.

It is necessary to be honest and acknowledge the challenges that aging brings, but it is also necessary to recognize and respect ourselves for dealing with those challenges. In his book, *Aging Well,* George E. Vaillant, MD (who was the director of the Harvard Study of Adult Development for thirty years), writes that "it is all right to be ill as long as you don't feel sick." This is a powerful statement, because it separates two things we believe to be inseparable.

What makes the difference? Having community, close friends, and interests that excite and engage us are all essential. So is laughter. Feeling good, being happy—maybe not 100 percent of the time but some of the time—not only benefits us on so many levels, but it is also the finest gift we can give the next generation.

In his chapter on Positive Aging, Vaillant refers to the AA watchwords, such as "Let go and let God," "First things first," and "Keep it simple." These familiar refrains are important at any age but essential as we move into old age.

Death

Death is absolutely safe. Nobody ever fails it.
—Ram Dass

At the Second Saturn Return, death enters the conversation; but at eighty, death dominates the conversation. There's nowhere else to put it; it's right there against you, and you can feel its breath on your skin. You cannot turn away. Maybe that's not such a bad thing. Having a better relationship with death takes away some of the fear and dread.

In many cultures, death is an integral part of life. The Irish are traditionally very hospitable to death. There is great support from the neighbors and the community and, of course, the Irish tradition of the wake. In Mexico, they celebrate the Day of the Dead. Our own Halloween has its roots in a Celtic festival of the dead. In New Orleans, they have the jazz funeral, a boisterous musical procession that combines West African, French, and African American traditions.

In our modern culture, death has been relegated to the very end of life, the outer edge of consciousness, so not to interfere with our busy lives. But whenever we push something out of awareness, we give it a negative power and disconnect from its real potential, then find an artificial or distorted way to replace it. Perhaps that's why we have so many violent movies and video games and our obsession with vampires and zombies.

I believe this is changing. The aging population combined with the concern for the environment, a commitment to the end of life, and the rapid growth of the hospice movement has created the perfect storm for this transition in how we view the death. The interest in Death Cafés, where people meet to discuss the end of life, is making a real difference. Green funerals that have a minimal environmental impact are becoming more popular, and there are improvements in hospice care.

The February 22, 2016, *Time* magazine's Longevity Issue posed the question: Why are old people less scared of dying? "You'd think people would get more anxious as they age," says Thomas Pyszcynski, professor at the University of Colorado. "But if you look at the research, older people have less anxiety and sadness and more overall satisfaction." Being closer to the end of life changes one's perspective. So does letting go of attachments.

It's Never Too Late to Fall in Love

Age puzzles me. I thought it was a quiet time. My seventies were interesting and fairly serene, but my eighties are passionate. I grow more intense as I age.
—Florida Scott-Maxwell

It's happening everywhere, in retirement communities, on cruises, in coffee shops, and especially online; in fact, the over-sixty crowd is the fastest growing group. Eve Pell was sixty-eight when she met Sam Hirabayshi, seventy-eight, who was in her running club. They fell in love and got married.

Eve wrote her story for the *New York Times* "Modern Love" column. The amount of response to her story caused Eve realize that there were lots of people her age falling in love. *Love, Again* is her book about her own late-in-life romance, as well as the experiences of many others.

Five Honeymoons

Evelyn De Wolfe was born and raised in Brazil. She left when she was twenty-one and set off to travel the world. Along the way, she became an author and a journalist, ultimately settling in southern California. For forty years, she worked for the *Los Angeles Times*.

She had been widowed for fourteen years, had grown children, grandchildren, and a full life. She was in good health and living contentedly in Hollywood, California. "What better place to be at eighty-two," she wrote, in her book *Five Honeymoons: A True Love Story*.

Then something unexpected happened. She received a mysterious envelope in the mail from her childhood sweetheart, and life suddenly took an astonishing turn. Juan had been her first real crush at age thirteen. She hadn't seen or heard from him for over sixty-five years. Like her, he was in his eighties, also with grown children, but he had remained in Brazil. An old friend had put them in touch, and Evelyn and Juan began emailing.

It wasn't long before they fell in love and began a passionate affair. But that isn't the most amazing part of the story; it's the form their affair took that makes it unique. Every year for five years they met in a different romantic location: a farm tucked away in the rain forest, Santa Barbara, Mexico, Hollywood, and Rio de Janeiro. *Five Honeymoons* is the story of their love affair and the precious moments spent together.

Betty Halbreich

If you're eighty-five and still working, you become interesting.
—Betty Halbreich

Betty Halbreich is the preeminent personal shopper at New York City's upscale Bergdorf Goodman department store, where she dresses the rich and powerful, celebrities and ordinary people alike and consults on movies and television shows like *Sex and the City*. Her style is legendary and so is her brassy, no-nonsense attitude. She has become a celebrity herself.

I relished her memoir, *I'll Drink to That*, about growing up in a wealthy Jewish family in Chicago, living a sheltered life, then getting married and coming to New York. She didn't work until the 1960s; in fact, she got her first job at her midlife, around age forty. Her only credentials were her superb style, which was the best possible calling card. She landed at Bergdorf and has been there ever since. "I work five days a week, from 8:30 a.m. to 5:00 p.m. It means I don't have to stay home. It gives me a destination and a voice."

You're Not Old Until You're Ninety

Rebecca Latimer wrote a delightful book called *You're Not Old Until You're Ninety*. Married to a diplomat, Rebecca has lived all over the world, but she didn't really wake up until she was sixty. According to her, she was loaded with fears and inhibitions. It wasn't until she and her husband moved to a small redwood house in New Hampshire that she began to "listen to the small voice inside me." She not only listened, she studied, learned, mediated, and she transformed. She recorded her personal journey in her book, which was published when she was ninety-two. Rebecca Latimer is the embodiment of conscious aging.

Norman Lear, perhaps the greatest comedy producer of all time, is hard at work trying to get a new television show off the ground. It's entitled *Guess Who Died?*—and is a show about the elderly. Lear is ninety-four. In a recent documentary about him and the show, he said, "Often I get undressed, look at myself nude—dissatisfied but amused—and I sing and dance in front of a full length mirror. And I have wondered for a great many years, how do we know that that's not the secret to longevity?"

Diana Vreeland, the famous editor and fashion doyenne, is someone else who stayed vital and relevant up until the end of her life. Many years ago, I read an interview with her. In it, she was asked what she thought of punk rock. "I like punk; it has energy!" she exclaimed. That got my attention, especially since she was in her eighties, and I was in my thirties!

I disliked punk back then. I hadn't explored it at all, I'm ashamed to say; it was pure prejudice on my part. After reading that interview, I thought to myself, if *she* can find something positive in it, then so can I. We don't have to love or embrace everything, but we owe it to ourselves to at least be willing to explore it, taste it, and try it before we form an opinion.

The important thing is not to stop questioning. Curiosity has its own reason for existing. One cannot help but be in awe when he contemplates the mysteries of eternity, of life, of the marvelous structures of reality. It is enough if one tries merely to comprehend a little of this mystery every day. Never lose a holy curiosity.
—Albert Einstein

Ending

Keep learning, listening, living fully, and loving deeply. Keep an open mind and an open heart. Trust your process. Don't be afraid to be who you are. Celebrate yourself, your life, and your age. Above all, be grateful—*no matter what is going on.*

The only question left to ask is, "Did you become yourself?" Did you grow, evolve, explore, and experiment? Did you learn something? Success can take many forms—a wonderful marriage or partnership, raising a family, creating close friendships, finding your calling, healing, being of service, making a contribution. *You don't have to have a big life to be a big person. You have only to be yourself— fully, deeply, passionately.*

And if you still haven't? Begin now. As long as you are alive and you have a desire to do something or learn something, it's still possible. That's the beauty of life; at any moment, we can wake up, transform, and start over. It's never, *ever* too late.

APPENDIX
Profiles

I have singled out Georgia O'Keeffe and Carl Jung, because they both lived long lives, and, like most renowned people, they made strong responses to their birth charts in very powerful and public ways.

Georgia O'Keeffe's cycles are clearly defined, and, being a public figure, there is a great deal of information about her. Since no exact birth time is available, I've made a "solar chart" calculated for dawn on the day she was born.

Carl Jung was a brilliant psychiatrist and psychotherapist, whose interests and contributions embraced both the scientific and the mystical. His chart clearly expresses that.

Georgia O'Keeffe

Georgia O'Keeffe was born in Sun Prairie, Wisconsin, on November 15, 1887, on the New Moon in Scorpio. On that day, both the Sun (identity, self, willpower) and Moon (heart and soul), as well as Mercury (communication and information) and Jupiter (faith, confidence, wealth), were in Pluto-ruled Scorpio, the sign of birth, death, sex, and transformation. Boil Scorpio down to one word: *intensity.* Some other words are single-minded, driven, focused, jealous, controlling, and passionate.

Scorpios are not known for moderation; they love and hate with equal ardor. With so much energy in one area, O'Keeffe could climb any mountain—but it had to be the right one. Clearly it was! She decided she wanted to be an artist at age ten and never wavered. Not once did she take another job; everything she did was in the service of her art. Georgia O'Keeffe may have been born in 1887 in a farmhouse in the tiny town of Sun Prairie, Wisconsin, but she seems to have given birth to herself.

Georgia O'Keeffe
Natal Chart
Nov 15 1887 NS, Tue
6:30 am CST +6:00
Sun Prairie, Wisconsin
43°N11'01" 089°W12'49"
Geocentric
Tropical
Placidus
Mean Node

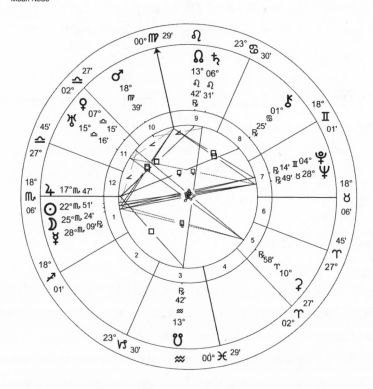

A *stellium* is a cluster of four or more planets in a sign or house. With those planets in uncompromising Scorpio, O'Keeffe's life was not about balance; it was about passion, devotion, and an obsessive allegiance to her calling. She would naturally radiate a strong presence and confidence, especially with giant Jupiter involved, but in deep, dark Scorpio, that demeanor would have been severe, even intimidating.

With any stellium, the opposite sign becomes essential; a place to release and express the tremendous energy. Taurus (opposite Scorpio) is the sign associated with beauty and nature; it is lush, carnal, and erotic, as well as deeply healing. We see it expressed in O'Keeffe's paintings of giant flowers, in the lavish colors, and in the stark landscape of the desert. Throughout her life, nature provided inspiration, pleasure, and solace.

Mystical Neptune, in Taurus, is opposite her Mercury, and Sun and Moon emphasize this. Although not religious, she found her own form of spirituality in the sanctuary of the desert. She created a magical world with her paintings and drew us all into it.

Venus, goddess of love, beauty, and relationship, resides in its home sign, elegant Libra. It makes a wide conjunction to free-spirited Uranus (also in Libra), showing O'Keeffe's need for autonomy; she craved intimacy and intensity, but she was also a loner who was fiercely independent.

Her Saturn, in creative Leo, gives her a powerful need for self-expression, as well as recognition and control. With Saturn here, there is often a love/hate relationship with the public and fame. It makes sense; she was famous for being private and a loner.

From 1901 to 1902, O'Keeffe attended high school at Sacred Heart Academy as a boarder. Although her parents relocated to Williamsburg, Virginia, in late 1902, O'Keeffe remained with her aunt in Wisconsin. O'Keeffe joined her parents in 1903. In 1905, she moved to Chicago to attend the School of the Art Institute of Chicago; she was eighteen at the time. In 1907, she relocated to New York City to study with William Merritt Chase at the Art Student League on 57th Street. O'Keeffe rented a room in a nearby rooming house. Mind you, this was 1907 and not 2007; it wasn't the custom for a young woman of twenty to arrive in New York City unchaperoned.

Uranus Square: When O'Keeffe was twenty-one, the time of her first Uranus square Uranus, she abandoned art—a radical move typical of Uranus. She decided that she couldn't express herself and did not paint for four years. So what did she do? She didn't get a job in a shop or as a nanny, nor did she marry. She returned to Chicago and worked as a commercial artist. She waited; she bided her time.

In 1912, O'Keeffe decided to go the University of Virginia's summer school and was re-inspired by Alon Bement, who introduced her to the work of Arthur Wesley Dow. From 1914 to 1915, she took classes from Dow at Columbia University; in the summer she served as his teaching assistant. In the fall of 1915, she took a job teaching at Columbia college in Columbia, South Carolina.

From 1916 to February of 1918, O'Keeffe worked as head of the art department at West Texas Normal College in the little town of Canyon, south of Amarillo. She was indifferent to the small town customs and made little effort to socialize. People thought her odd; she dressed in black, wore her hair pulled back in a tight knot, and when she wasn't teaching, she spent hours painting in the prairie or walking great distances—even at night.

Saturn Return: O'Keeffe had done some charcoal drawings in late 1915, which she sent to her friend Anita Pollitzer. It was Pollitzer who took them to Alfred Stieglitz at his 291 gallery in early 1916. He told Pollitzer that the drawings were "the purest, finest, sincerest things that had entered 291 in a long while." Steiglitz exhibited them without O'Keeffe's permission.

When O'Keeffe found out, she went to New York and confronted him. This was the first time they had met in person. She was twenty-nine years old. In April 1917, Steiglitz organized O'Keeffe's first solo show. They fell madly in love and married in 1924, when O'Keeffe was thirty-seven, at her Saturn square. Stieglitz organized annual exhibitions of her work, and by the mid-1920s, O'Keeffe had become one of America's most important and well-known artists.

Midlife: O'Keeffe felt increasingly stifled by New York City, as well as Lake George, where she and Stieglitz spent the summers surrounded by his family and friends. By 1929, she needed to find a source of new inspiration. In May 1929, she traveled to Santa Fe by train with her friend Rebecca Strand. Shortly after they arrived, Mable Dodge Luhan (a patron of the arts) moved them to Taos and even provided them with studios. That summer, O'Keeffe explored the rugged mountains and deserts in the region, where she completed her famous oil painting, *The Lawrence Tree.* This was no ordinary trip, no ordinary land; this was a love affair—she had found her muse and her home. Between 1929 and 1949, she spent a part of every year working in New Mexico

Chiron Return: In 1939, O'Keeffe was given a commission from an advertising agency to create two paintings for Hawaiian Pineapple Company (now Dole Food Company) and was sent to Hawaii for nine weeks. After a year of constant travel (New York,

New Mexico, California, and Hawaii), she returned exhausted and tense, and her doctors ordered her to remain in bed and advised her not to travel. By the end of the summer, she had begun to recover. During that same period, O'Keeffe, along with achievers such as Eleanor Roosevelt and Hellen Keller, was named one of the twelve most outstanding women of the past fifty years.

In August 1934, she visited Ghost Ranch north of Abiqui, saw it, and decided immediately to buy it. In 1940, at the end of her Chiron Return, she moved in. It was this land that inspired her most important landscapes.

Second Saturn Return: Alfred Stieglitz died on July 13, 1946, when O'Keeffe was fifty-nine, at the time of her Second Saturn Return. They had been together for thirty years—a full Saturn cycle. She spent the next three years mostly in New York, resolving his estate and preparing for the next chapter of her life.

The Closing Uranus Square: In 1949 (at age sixty-two), she returned to New Mexico permanently. It was at her Uranus opposition at age forty-two that she had discovered New Mexico; now she was going back at the closing square.

Uranus Return: In 1970 (at age eighty-three), O'Keeffe had her Uranus return; Uranus returned to its natal position in Libra, the sign that rules beauty and art. It was fitting that the Whitney Museum of American Art mounted the Georgia O'Keeffe Retrospective Exhibition. This was the first retrospective of her work in New York since 1946, the year Stieglitz died, and it did a great deal to revive her career.

The Story Doesn't End There: In 1973, a young potter named Juan Hamilton appeared at the ranch house looking for work. She hired him to do a few odd jobs; eventually, she employed him full time. Hamilton became her closest confidant, companion, and business manager. O'Keeffe's eyesight was failing (she had macular degeneration), but Hamilton taught her to work with clay; with assistance, she produced clay pots and a series of water colors. In 1976, she even wrote a book about her art; the following year, she allowed a film to be made about her. She died March 6, 1986, at the age of ninety-eight.

Georgia O'Keeffe lived fully, passionately, and intensely right up until the end. That doesn't mean it was always easy or smooth, but she followed her calling and manifested it unequivocally. "I have been absolutely terrified every moment of my life, but I never let it keep me from doing a single thing I wanted to do," she said.

Carl Gustav Jung

Carl Jung was born on July 26, 1875, at 7:32 p.m. in Kesswil, Switzerland. His Sun is in proud and charismatic Leo in the 6th house of work, health, service, and mentoring. His Moon is in sensual Taurus in the 3rd house, the area that rules communication, information, writing, and teaching. His rising sign is Aquarius, the rebel, the outsider, the nonconformist.

Both the Sun and the Moon are in their natural signs; the Sun rules Leo, the Moon rules Taurus. This gives him a strong and imposing physique and a powerful presence—magnetic, hearty, stubborn, and vigorous; someone with large appetites and a deep love of nature and the natural world.

There are two distinct themes in his chart. On one hand, he was a maverick, an eccentric, and a genius. We see that in the Aquarius ascendant and the fact that his earthy Taurus Moon makes a square to unconventional Uranus—the planet that rules Aquarius, the planet of freedom and individuation. No wonder he broke with Freud; he was a pioneer, not a follower.

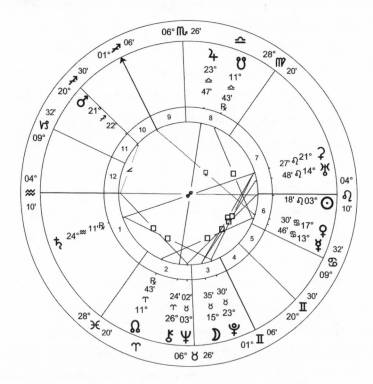

Carl Jung
Natal Chart
Jul 26 1875 NS, Mon
7:32 pm −0:29:44
Kesswil, Switzerland
47°N36' 009°E20'
Geocentric
Tropical
Placidus
Mean Node

On the other hand, he was conservative and down to earth; someone with a strong work ethic and tremendous staying power. That shows up in Saturn, the planet of responsibility and discipline, in Aquarius in the first house of the self. He may have given the impression of someone who was progressive, but at the same time, he radiated a powerful sense of duty and dependability. Plus, his Leo Sun is in the 6th house of work, competence, and skill. He was a serious rebel, an eccentric conservative; someone who moved freely in both worlds, equally at home in the psychoanalytical one in Switzerland, as well as in esoteric circles.

In addition, his Leo Sun makes a tight square to Neptune, the planet of spirituality and mysticism. Neptune dissolves the boundaries between the visible and invisible worlds; from an early age Jung was drawn to the occult and séances. Both Sun and Moon are connected to outer or transpersonal planets; it's no surprise that he studied alchemy, he was passionate about astrology in his practice, and he worked with mythology and dreams.

Pluto is in Taurus is in the third house of the mind. He had a deep and penetrating intellect and was a gifted speaker and prolific writer. We also see that in the conjunction of mental Mercury and lovely Venus (beautiful words). His Mars in the public tenth house brought a fierce ambition. Jupiter in the eighth house (the natural home of Scorpio) gave him a deep faith and a fascination for those parts of ourselves that we bury in our subconscious. Although he didn't invent the *Shadow,* he coined the term.

Carl Jung's life and his work can be seen clearly in his birth chart. He was someone who wasn't afraid to break boundaries, cut ties, and challenge the status quo. His ideas were revolutionary, yet those groundbreaking concepts were anchored in a solid framework, a psychological and spiritual system. His greatest contributions were the Jungian archetypes, the process of individuation, the collective unconscious, synchronicity, etc. He created a new language—one that we are still speaking today.

SUGGESTED READING

Books
General Astrology
The Astrology Sourcebook, by Shirley Soffer (Lowell House, 1998).

Cosmos and Psyche, by Richard Tarnas (Viking Penguin, 2006).

The Gods of Change, by Howard Sasportas (Arkana/Penguin Group, 1989).

Images of Soul: Reimagining Astrology, by Hadley Fitzgerald, and Judith Harte (Iris & Acorn Press, 2014).

The Inner Sky and *The Changing Sky,* by Steven Forrest (Seven Paws Press, 2007 and 2008).

Making the Gods Work for You: The Astrological Language of the Psyche, by Caroline W. Casey (Harmony Books, 1998).

Planetary Cycles, by Betty Lundsted Samuel (Weiser, Inc., 1984).

Secrets from a Stargazer's Notebook, by Debbi Kempton-Smith (Topquark Press, 1999).

The Saturn Return
Astrology, Karma, and Transformation, by Stephen Arroyo (CRCS Publications, 1992).

Saturn: A New Look at an Old Devil, by Liz Green (Red Wheel/Weiser, 1976).

Saturn Cycles: Mapping Changes in Your Life, by Wendell C. Perry (Llewellyn, 2009).

Saturn Returns: The Private Papers of a Reluctant Astrologer, by Elizabeth Spring (self-published, 2011).

Midlife
The Age of Miracles: Embracing the New Midlife, by Marianne Williamson (Hay House, 2008).

The Art of Stillness: Adventures in Going Nowhere, by Pico Iyer (Simon & Schuster/TED, 2014).

The Astrology of Midlife and Aging, by Erin Sullivan (Jeremy P. Tarcher/Penguin, 2005).

Broken Open: How Difficult Times Can Help Us Grow, by Elizabeth Lesser (Villard, 2004).

The Dark Side of the Light Chasers, by Debbie Ford (Riverhead Books, 1998).

In Midlife: Finding Meaning in the Second Half of Life, by James Hollis (Gotham Books, 2006).

Passages: Predictable Crises of Adult Life, by Gail Sheehy (Bantam Books, 1976).

The Second Half of Life: Opening the Eight Gates of Wisdom, by Angeles Arrien (Sounds True, 2005).

The Way of Transition, by William Bridges (Perseus Publishing, 2001).

When Things Fall Apart, by Pema Chödrön (Shambala, 2000).

The Chiron Return and the Fifties

Chiron: The Healing Journey, by Melanie Reinhart (Starwalker Press, 2009).

Facing Our Fifties, by Peter A. O'Connor (Allen & Unwin, 2000).

The Gifts of Imperfection, by Brene Brown (Hazelden, 2010).

The Liquid Light of Sex: Kundalini, Astrology, and the Key Life Transitions, by Barbara Hand Clow (Bear & Company, 1991).

My Time: Making the Most of the Bonus Decades after Fifty, by Abigail Trafford (Basic Books, 2004).

Revolution from Within, by Gloria Steinem (Little, Brown and Company, 1992).

The Wisdom of Menopause, by Christiane Northrup, MD (Bantam Books, 2001).

The Second Saturn Return

Age-ing to Sage-ing: A Profound New Vision of Growing Older, by Zalman Schachter-Shalomi, and Ronald S. Miller (Warner Books, 1995).

Conscious Living, Conscious Aging, by Ron Pevny (Atria Books/Beyond Words, 2014).

Finding Meaning in the Second Half of Life, by James Hollis (Penguin Group, 2006).

Prime Time: Love, Health, Sex, Fitness, Friendship, Spirit, by Jane Fonda (Random House, 2011).

Thrive: The Third Metric to Redefining Success and Creating a Life of Well-Being, Wisdom, and Wonder, by Arianna Huffington (Harmony Books, 2014).

The Uranus Square and the Sixties

Crones Don't Whine, by Jean Shinola Bolen (Conari Press, 2003).

The Goddesses in Older Women: Archetypes in Women over Fifty, by Jean Shinoda Bolen (Quill/Harper Collins, 2001).

How to Age, by Anne Karpf (Macmillan, 2014).

Moving Beyond Words, by Gloria Steinem (Simon & Schuster, 1994).

Still Foolin' 'Em: Where I've Been, Where I'm Going, and Where the Hell Are My Keys? by Billy Crystal (St. Martin's Press, 2014).

Still Here: Embracing Aging, Changing, and Dying, by Ram Dass (Riverhead Books, 2000).

The Seventies and Health

Aging Well, by George Valliant, MD (Little Brown and Company, 2003).

At Seventy, by May Sarton (W. W. Norton & Company, 1984).

The Creative Age: Awakening Human Potential in the Second Half of Life, by Gene D. Cohen, MD (Quill/Harper Collins, 2000).

Goddesses Never Age, by Christiane Northrup (Hay House, 2015).

It Takes a Long Time to Become Young, by Richard Kehl (Darling & Company, 2008).

The Journey through Cancer, by Jeremy Geffen, MD (Harmony, 2006).

The Mind Body Code: How to Change the Beliefs that Limit Your Health, Longevity, and Success, by Dr. Mario Martinez (Sounds True, 2014).

Super Brain, by Deepak Chopra, MD, and Rudolph E. Tanzi, PhD (Three Rivers Press, 2012).

When Food Is Love, by Geneen Roth (Penguin Group, 1992).

You Can Heal Your Life, by Louise Hay (Hay House, 1984).

The Uranus Return and the Eighties

Anam Cara: A Book of Celtic Wisdom, by John O'Donohue (Harper Perennial, 1997).

Fate and Destiny: The Two Agreements of the Soul, by Michael Meade (Green-Fire Press, 2012).

The Gift of Years, by Joan Chittister (Blue Bridge, 2008).

I'll Drink to That, by Betty Halbreich (Penguin Press, 2014).

The Lavender Lace Bra: Wisdom Thoughts on Aging Beautifully, by Ilene Cummings (self-published, 2009).

The Measure of My Days, by Florida Scott-Maxwell (Alfred A. Knopf, 1968).

Memories, Dreams, Reflections, by C. G. Jung (Vintage Books, 1989).

My Life on the Road, by Gloria Steinem (Random House, 2015).

You're Not Old until You're Ninety, by Rebecca Latimer (Blue Dolphin Publishing, 1996).

CDs

The Crown of Age: The Rewards of Conscious Aging, by Marion Woodman.

The Dangerous Old Woman, by Clarissa Pinkola Estés, PhD.

Finding Genius in Your Life, by Michael Meade.

Midlife and the Great Unknown, by David Whyte.

Seeing in the Dark, by Clarissa Pinkola Estés, PhD.

Films

Diana Vreeland: The Eye Has to Travel

Fierce Grace

Harold and Maude

Iris (a documentary about Iris Apfel)

ABOUT THE AUTHOR

 Virginia Bell has been a fulltime astrologer since the 1990s, and currently writes a horoscope column and celebrity profiles for the CBS magazine, *Watch!* She's a regular contributor to the *Huffington Post* and has written astrology columns for magazines including *TV Guide* and *US Weekly*. Visit Virginia online at *www.virginiabellastrology.com.*

To Our Readers

Weiser Books, an imprint of Red Wheel/Weiser, publishes books across the entire spectrum of occult, esoteric, speculative, and New Age subjects. Our mission is to publish quality books that will make a difference in people's lives without advocating any one particular path or field of study. We value the integrity, originality, and depth of knowledge of our authors.

Our readers are our most important resource, and we appreciate your input, suggestions, and ideas about what you would like to see published.

Visit our website at *www.redwheelweiser.com* to learn about our upcoming books and free downloads, and be sure to go to *www.redwheelweiser.com/newsletter* to sign up for newsletters and exclusive offers.

You can also contact us at *info@rwwbooks.com* or at

Red Wheel/Weiser, LLC
65 Parker Street, Suite 7
Newburyport, MA 01950